COPYCAT RECIPES

THE ULTIMATE COOKBOOK FOR MAKING YOUR FAVOURITE RESTAURANT DISHES AT HOME, INCLUDING DELICIOUS, QUICK AND EASY TO FOLLOW RECIPES

OLIVIA HOWARD

© Copyright 2019 by Olivia Howard All rights reserved.

This document is geared towards providing exact and reliable information in regards to the topic and issue covered. The publication is sold with the idea that the publisher is not required to render accounting, officially permitted, or otherwise, qualified services. If advice is necessary, legal or professional, a practiced individual in the profession should be ordered.

- From a Declaration of Principles which was accepted and approved equally by a Committee of the American Bar Association and a Committee of Publishers and Associations.

In no way is it legal to reproduce, duplicate, or transmit any part of this document in either electronic means or in printed format. Recording of this publication is strictly prohibited and any storage of this document is not allowed unless with written permission from the publisher. All rights reserved.

The information provided herein is stated to be truthful and consistent, in that any liability, in terms of inattention or otherwise, by any usage or abuse of any policies, processes, or directions contained within is the solitary and utter responsibility of the recipient reader. Under no circumstances will any legal responsibility or blame be held against the publisher for any reparation, damages, or monetary loss due to the information herein, either directly or indirectly.

Respective authors own all copyrights not held by the publisher.

The information herein is offered for informational purposes solely, and is universal as so. The presentation of the information is without contract or any type of guarantee assurance.

TABLE OF CONTENTS

Introduction to Copycat Recipes 1

Chapter 1: Copycat Breakfast Recipes 2

Chapter 2: Copycat Lunch Recipes 28

Chapter 3: Copycat Dinner Recipes 64

Chapter 4: Copycat Dessert Recipes 95

Conclusion 130

INTRODUCTION TO COPYCAT RECIPES

Thank you for downloading our copycat cookbook. Cooking at home has many benefits, for example saving money, time, controlling portion sizing, and customizing each meal.

In this book, you will find tips on how to create restaurant dishes at home. You'll be surprised at how simple some of them are to make. Many of our best-loved restaurants use classic recipes with jazzed up names to tickle our appetite.

Restaurants usually choose recipes that are easy to make and that make use of simple ingredients, so you'll find that many of them are convenient to prepare in your own kitchen. Of course, there are some more intricate recipes, but the results are well worth it.

CHAPTER 1:
COPYCAT BREAKFAST RECIPES

DIY CALIFORNIA A.M. CRUNCHWRAP

Preparation Time: 10 minutes
Cooking Time: 20-30 minutes

Ingredients:
- 4 frozen hash browns
- 5 large eggs
- 1 tbsp milk
- salt and pepper
- 4 large tortillas
- 1 cup cheddar cheese, shredded
- 4 strips of thick cut bacon, cooked and crumbled
- 2 ripe avocados, peeled and pitted
- 4 tbsp pico de gallo

Directions:
1. Cook hash browns until crisp, based on package instructions.
2. Add eggs, milk, salt, and pepper in a bowl. Mix well until combined. Then, pour into a skillet and cook until scrambled. Set aside.
3. Heat one small and one larger pan over medium heat. Once heated, place a tortilla into the large pan and in even amounts, add cheese, a hash brown, eggs, bacon, avocado, and pico de gallo in the center of the tortilla.
4. Using a wheel pattern, fold tortilla around the filling with the edge facing up. Place the heated smaller pan on top for about 20 seconds or until browned.

PANERA SPINACH AND CHEESE EGG SOUFFLÉ

Preparation Time: 15 minutes

Cooking Time: 25 minutes

Ingredients:
- 1 tube butter flaky crescent rolls
- 6 eggs, divided
- 2 tbsp milk
- 2 tbsp heavy cream
- 1/4 cup cheddar cheese, grated
- 1/4 cup jack cheese, grated
- 1 tbsp parmesan cheese
- 3 tbsp fresh spinach, chopped
- 4 slices of bacon, cooked and crumbled
- cooking spray
- salt
- 1/4 cup Asiago cheese, grated

Directions:
1. Preheat oven to 375 degrees F.
2. Add 5 eggs, milk, heavy cream, cheddar cheese, jack cheese, parmesan cheese, spinach, bacon, and salt to a microwave safe bowl.
3. Mix well until combined then heat in microwave for about 30 seconds. Stir, then microwave for another 20 seconds. Repeat 5 times until egg mixture is a thicker but still runny and uncooked.
4. Roll out crescent roll dough. Make 4 rectangles by pressing together the triangles. Then, using a roll pin, stretch them out until they are 6x6 inch square.

5. Coat ramekin with cooking spray and place flattened roll inside, making sure the edges are outside the ramekin. Add 1/3 cup egg mixture and then add 1/4 of the Asiago cheese. Wrap edges to seal. Repeat for remaining rolls.
6. Whisk remaining egg with salt lightly in a bowl. Brush on each roll.
7. Place ramekins in the oven and bake for 20 minutes or until brown.

MCDONALD'S' FRUIT AND YOGURT PARFAIT

Preparation Time: 5 minutes

Ingredients:
- 6 oz vanilla yogurt
- 4–6 strawberries, sliced
- 1/4 cup blueberries, fresh or frozen
- 1/4 cup pecans, chopped

Directions:
1. Place 2 ounces of vanilla yogurt at the bottom of a cup, followed by 2–3 strawberries and 1/8 cup each of blueberries and pecans.
2. Place another layer of yogurt, strawberries, blueberries, and pecans on top of the first layer.
3. Finish off the parfait with the remaining yogurt.

PANERA BREAD'S CINNAMON CRUNCH BAGEL

Preparation Time: 1 hour
Cooking Time: 25 minutes

Ingredients:

For the bread:

- 1 1/4 cups warm water
- 1 tbsp yeast
- 1 tbsp salt
- 4 tbsp honey
- 1 1/2 cups whole wheat pastry flour
- 1/2 tbsp cinnamon
- 1 3/4 cups bread flour
- 3/4 cup white chocolate chips
- cornmeal, for sprinkling
- 20 cups water

For the topping:

- 1/4 cup granulated sugar
- 1/4 cup packed brown sugar
- 1 tbsp cinnamon
- 1/3 cup coconut oil

Directions:

1. Activate the yeast by mixing it with the warm water and setting it aside for 10 minutes.
2. Add in 3 tbsp honey, salt, pastry flour, and cinnamon. Mix all the ingredients together with a wooden spoon. After a minute of mixing, or when the flour is fully incorporated, scrape the sides of the bowl and mix again for another minute.

3. Let the dough rest for 5 minutes, if lumps form, stir the batter to break them apart.
4. Add in half a cup of bread flour and start kneading. Keep adding the bread flour half a cup at a time while kneading the dough to distribute the flour throughout.
5. After about seven minutes of kneading, add in the white chocolate chips and continue kneading to completely incorporate the chips into the mixture.
6. Cover the bowl with a towel and leave to rest for one hour.
7. After an hour, flour a flat surface. Transfer the dough from its bowl to the floured surface and punch it down.
8. Cut the dough into 8 equal pieces. Roll them into ropes. Let the dough rest again, for 3 to 4 minutes.
9. Form a circle with each piece of dough, twisting the ends securely together. Sprinkle a baking sheet with cornmeal and place the dough circles on the sheet. Cover with a towel and let rest for 10 to 15 minutes.
10. Bring the water to a boil. When the water is boiling, add the remaining 1 tbsp of honey. Keep the water at a low boil.
11. After 15 minutes, place a few dough circles into the boiling water. Leave them to cook for 50 seconds on each side.
12. Preheat the oven to 450 degrees F. Line a baking sheet with parchment or wax paper.
13. Mix the topping ingredients, except the oil, together.
14. When boiled, transfer them to the baking sheet using a slotted spoon so as to drain off the water.
15. When all have boiled, brush each one with coconut oil and sprinkle with the sugar mixture.
16. Bake for 20 to 25 minutes, then transfer to a wire rack to let them cool.

IHOP'S BUTTERMILK PANCAKE

Preparation Time: 5 minutes
Cooking Time: 8 minutes

Ingredients:

- 1 1/4 cups all-purpose flour
- 1 tsp baking soda
- 1 tsp baking powder
- 1 1/4 cups granulated sugar
- pinch of salt
- 1 egg
- 1 1/4 cups buttermilk
- 1/4 cup cooking oil
- maple syrup, for garnishing

Directions:

1. Preheat your pan by leaving it over medium heat while you are preparing the pancake batter.
2. Take all of the dry ingredients and mix them together.
3. Take all of the wet ingredients, except maple syrup and oil, and mix them together.
4. Carefully combine the dry mixture with the wet mixture until everything is mixed together.
5. Melt oil in the pan.
6. Slowly pour batter into the pan until you have a 5 inch circle.
7. Flip the pancake when the edges have hardened.
8. Cook the other side of the pancake until it is golden brown.
9. Serve with maple syrup.

MCDONALD'S BREAKFAST BURRITO

Preparation Time: 10 minutes

Cooking Time: 16 minutes

Ingredients:
- 1/2 lb bulk sausage, cooked and crumbled
- 10 eggs
- 1 medium tomato, diced
- 1 small onion, diced
- 3 tbsp canned green chili, diced
- salt and pepper
- butter
- 10 flour tortillas, warm
- 10 slices American cheese, halved
- salsa, for garnishing
- sour cream, for garnishing

Directions:
1. Mix the sausage, eggs, tomato, onion, chili, salt, and pepper together in a medium-sized bowl.
2. Butter a non-stick pan over medium heat.
3. Pour the mixture into the pan and then cook until the egg is cooked through.
4. Lay out the tortillas and start assembling the burritos by placing 1/10 of the mixture in each of the tortillas.
5. Place the cheese on top of the egg mixture, then roll up the tortilla to make the burrito.
6. Garnish with salsa and sour cream.

STARBUCKS'S MARBLE POUND CAKE

Preparation Time: 10 minutes

Cooking Time: 1 hour 30 minutes

Ingredients:

- 4 1/2 cups cake flour + extra for lining
- 2 tsp baking powder
- 1/8 tsp salt
- 6 oz semisweet chocolate, finely chopped
- 2 cups unsalted butter, softened
- 3 cups granulated sugar
- 1 tbsp vanilla
- 1 lemon, grated for zest
- 10 large eggs
- 2 tbsp milk

Directions:

1. Preheat the oven to 350 degrees F, grease a 10×4 inch loaf pan, line the pan's bottom with greased wax paper and flour the entire pan.
2. Sift together the cake flour, baking powder, and salt in a medium-sized bowl.
3. Melt the chocolate in a medium-sized bowl, then beat in the butter. When the mixture is smooth, beat in the sugar, lemon zest, and vanilla until the liquid mixture is uniform.
4. When the mixture is fully beaten, beat in the eggs, 2 at a time, until the mixture looks curdled.
5. Pour half of the dry mixture into the liquid mixture and mix until blended.
6. Add the milk and the rest of the dry mixture. Continue beating the mixture.

7. When the mixture is blended, use a spatula to start folding it.
8. Set aside 4 cups of the batter. Whisk the melted chocolate into the remaining batter.
9. Now that you have a light batter and a dark batter, place the batter into the pan by the spoonful, alternating between the two colors.
10. When the pan is full, shake it slightly to level the batter. Run a knife through the batter to marble it.
11. Place the pan in the oven and bake for an hour and 15 minutes. Test with a toothpick. If there are still some moist crumbs on the toothpick when you take it out, then the cake is done.
12. Remove the cake from the pan and leave it to rest overnight.

IHOP'S SCRAMBLED EGG

Preparation Time: 5 minutes

Cooking Time: 5 minutes

Ingredients:

- 1/4 cup pancake mix
- 2 tbsp butter
- 6 large eggs
- salt and pepper

Directions:

1. Thoroughly beat the pancake mix and the eggs together until no lumps remain.
2. Butter a pan over medium heat.
3. When the pan is hot enough, pour the egg mixture in the middle of the pan.
4. Add the salt and pepper and let the mixture sit for about a minute.
5. When the egg starts cooking, start pushing the edges of the mixture toward the middle of the pan. Continue until the entire mixture is cooked.
6. Serve and enjoy.

MCDONALD'S SAUSAGE EGG MCMUFFIN

Preparation Time: 10 minutes

Cooking Time: 15 minutes

Ingredients:
- 4 English muffins, cut in half horizontally
- 4 slices American processed cheese
- 1/2 tbsp oil
- 1 lb ground pork, minced
- 1/2 tsp dried sage, ground
- 1/2 tsp dried thyme
- 1 tsp onion powder
- salt and pepper
- 1/2 tsp white sugar
- 4 large 1/3 inch onion ring slices
- 4 large eggs
- 2 tbsp water

Directions:
1. Preheat oven to 300 degrees F.
2. Cover half of the muffin with cheese, leaving one half uncovered. Transfer both halves to a baking tray. Place in oven.
3. For the sausage patties, use your hands to mix pork, sage, thyme, onion powder, pepper, salt, and sugar in a bowl. Form into 4 patties. Make sure they are slightly larger than the muffins.
4. Heat oil in a pan. Cook patties on both sides for at least 2 minutes each or until all sides turn brown.
5. Remove tray of muffins from oven. Place cooked sausage patties on top of the cheese on muffins. Return tray to the oven.

6. In the pan, position onion rings flat into a single layer. Crack one egg inside each of the onion rings to make them round. Add water carefully into the sides of the pan and cover. Cook for 2 minutes.
7. Remove tray of muffins from the oven. Add eggs on top of patties, then top with the other muffin half.

STARBUCKS' SPINACH AND FETA BREAKFAST WRAPS

Preparation Time: 5 minutes

Cooking Time: 20 minutes

Ingredients:
- 10 oz spinach leaves
- 1 can diced tomatoes, drained
- 3 tbsp cream cheese
- 10 egg whites
- 1/2 tsp oregano
- 1/2 tsp garlic salt
- 1/8 tsp pepper
- 6 whole wheat tortillas
- 4 tbsp feta cheese, crumbled
- cooking spray

Directions:
1. Apply a light coating of cooking spray to a pan. Cook spinach leaves on medium-high heat for 5 minutes or until leaves wilt, then stir in tomatoes and cream cheese. Cook for an additional 5 minutes or until cheese is melted completely. Remove from pan and place into glass bowl and cover. Set aside.
2. In the same pan, add egg whites, oregano, salt, and pepper. Stir well and cook at least 5 minutes or until eggs are scrambled. Remove from heat.
3. Microwave tortillas for 30 seconds or until warm. Place egg whites, spinach and tomato mixture, and feta in the middle of the tortillas. Fold sides inwards, like a burrito.
4. Serve.

JIMMY DEAN'S HOMEMADE PORK SAGE SAUSAGE

Preparation Time: 5 minutes

Cooking Time: 20 minutes

Ingredients:

- 1 lb ground pork
- 1 tsp salt
- 1/2 tsp dried parsley
- 1/4 tsp rubbed sage
- 1/4 tsp black pepper, ground
- 1/4 tsp dried thyme
- 1/4 tsp coriander
- 1/4 tsp seasoned salt

Directions:

1. Mix all ingredients in a bowl.
2. Shape into patties. Cook in a pan on medium heat until brown on both sides and cooked through.
3. Serve.

PANERA POWER BREAKFAST SANDWICH

Preparation Time: 10 minutes

Cooking Time: 7 minutes

Ingredients:
- 2 egg whites
- 1 tsp butter
- 1 bagel, cut in half
- mustard
- 1/4 avocado, sliced
- 1 large tomato slice
- 4 spinach leaves
- 1 slice Swiss cheese
- cooking spray

Directions:
1. Cook egg whites for about 1 minute in a small tightly covered cup in the microwave.
2. Apply 1/2 tsp butter onto both bagel halves.
3. Coat the inside of the top half of the bagel with mustard and the bottom with avocado. Place cooked egg whites, tomato, spinach leaves, and cheese on bottom bagel thin. Top with the other bagel half.
4. Coat a heated pan with thin layer of cooking spray, pan fry on medium-high heat for 3 minutes on each side or until golden brown and cheese is melted.

MCDONALD'S MCGRIDDLE BREAKFAST SANDWICH

Preparation Time: 1 hour

Cooking Time: 15 minutes

Ingredients:

- 1/2 cup maple syrup
- 1 cup flour
- 1 tsp baking powder
- 1/2 tsp baking soda
- 1 cup buttermilk
- 2 tbsp butter, melted + extra for greasing
- 1 egg
- 4 slices American cheese
- 4 eggs, scrambled
- 4 strips bacon, cooked and cut in half

Directions:

1. Line a baking tray with parchment paper and set aside.
2. Add maple syrup to a pot and bring to a boil over medium heat while stirring often. Continue stirring the syrup once boiling.
3. After about a minute of boiling, the syrup will appear a bit darker and the boiling will lessen to some degree.
4. Cook for about 2 more minutes or until syrup becomes darker and begins to smell like caramel. It is ready to be removed from heat once it reaches 265 degrees F.
5. Pour maple syrup onto the prepared baking sheet. Spread evenly in a thin layer with a spatula. Refrigerate until cool.
6. Once cool, flip the syrup over, with parchment paper now on top. Then, peel off the paper and break the solidified syrup into tiny pieces.

7. To make the pancakes, combine flour, baking powder, and baking soda in a large bowl. Set aside.
8. In another bowl, add buttermilk, butter, and egg. Mix together until fully combined. Then, pour into dry ingredients and mix well until incorporated.
9. Preheat griddle to medium high heat.
10. Coat insides of round molds with softened butter then place on a hot griddle over medium heat.
11. Add 2 tbsp pancake batter into each mold, sprinkle maple crystals on top, then add 2 more tbsp of pancake batter on top, sandwiching the maple crystals inside the pancakes.
12. Once bubbles form and edges look cooked, remove molds and flip pancakes. Cook for an additional 1 to 2 minutes.
13. To assemble the sandwiches, add cheese, scrambled egg, and bacon inbetween 2 pancakes.

STARBUCKS'S CHOCOLATE CINNAMON BREAD

Preparation Time: 15 minutes

Cooking Time: 1 hour

Ingredients:

For the bread:

- 1 1/2 cups unsalted butter
- 3 cups granulated sugar
- 5 large eggs
- 2 cups flour
- 1 1/4 cups processed cocoa
- 1 tbsp ground cinnamon
- 1 tsp salt
- 1/2 tsp baking powder
- 1/2 tsp baking soda
- 1/4 cup water
- 1 cup buttermilk
- 1 tsp vanilla extract

For the topping:

- 1/4 cup granulated sugar
- 1/2 tsp cinnamon
- 1/2 tsp processed cocoa
- 1/8 tsp ginger, ground
- 1/8 tsp cloves, ground

Directions:
1. Preheat the oven to 350 degrees F, grease 2 9×5×3 loaf pans and line the bottoms of the pans with wax paper.
2. Cream the sugar by beating it with the butter.
3. Beat the eggs into the mixture one at a time.
4. Sift the flour, cocoa, cinnamon, salt, baking powder, and baking soda into a large bowl.
5. In another bowl, whisk together the water, buttermilk, and vanilla.
6. Make a well in the dry mixture and start pouring in both wet mixtures a little at a time, while whisking.
7. When the mixture starts becoming doughy, divide it in 2 and transfer it to the pans.
8. Mix together all the topping ingredients and sprinkle evenly on top of the mixture.
9. Bake for 50 to 60 minutes, or until the bread has set.

STARBUCKS'S LEMON LOAF

Preparation Time: 15 minutes

Cooking Time: 45 minutes

Ingredients:

For the bread:

- 1 1/2 cups flour
- 1/2 tsp baking soda
- 1/2 tsp baking powder
- 1/2 tsp salt
- 1 cup sugar
- 3 eggs, room temperature
- 2 tbsp butter, softened
- 1 tsp vanilla extract
- 1/3 cup lemon juice
- 1/2 cup oil

For the icing:

- 1 cup + 1 tbsp powdered sugar
- 2 tbsp milk
- 1/2 tsp lemon extract

Directions:

1. Preheat the oven to 350 degrees F, grease and flour a 9×5×3 loaf pan, and line the pan's bottom with wax paper.
2. Mix the flour, baking soda, baking powder, and salt in a large bowl.
3. Beat the eggs, butter, vanilla, and lemon juice together in a medium bowl until the mixture becomes smooth.
4. Make a well in the middle of the dry mixture and pour the wet mixture into the well.

5. Mix everything together with a whisk or hand mixer. Add the oil. Do not stop mixing until everything is fully blended and smooth.
6. Pour the batter into the pan and bake for 45 minutes. Or until a toothpick comes out clean.
7. While the bread is baking, make the icing by mixing the icing ingredients in a small bowl using a whisk or hand mixer until smooth.
8. When the bread is done baking, place it on a cooling rack and leave it for at least 20 minutes to cool.
9. When the bread is cool enough, pour the icing over the top. Wait for the icing to set before slicing.

WAFFLE HOUSE'S WAFFLE

Preparation Time: 5 minutes
Chilling Time: 12 hours
Cooking Time: 20 minutes

Ingredients:

- 1 1/2 cups all-purpose flour
- 1 tsp salt
- 1/2 tsp baking soda
- 1 egg
- 1/2 cup + 1 tbsp granulated white sugar
- 2 tbsp butter, softened
- 2 tbsp shortening
- 1/2 cup half-and-half
- 1/2 cup milk
- 1/4 cup buttermilk
- 1/4 tsp vanilla
- maple syrup, for garnishing

Directions:

1. Prepare the dry mixture by sifting the flour into a bowl and mixing it with the salt and baking soda.
2. In a medium bowl, lightly beat an egg. When the egg has become frothy, beat in the butter, sugar, and shortening. When the mixture is thoroughly mixed, beat in the half-and-half, vanilla, milk, and buttermilk. Continue beating the mixture until smooth.
3. While beating the wet mixture, slowly pour in the dry mixture, making sure to mix thoroughly and remove all the lumps.
4. Chill the batter overnight.
5. Take the batter out of the refrigerator. Preheat and grease your waffle iron.
6. Cook each waffle for 3 to 4 minutes. Serve with syrup.

MIMI'S CAFÉ SANTA FÉ OMELET

Preparation Time: 10 minutes

Cooking Time: 10 minutes

Ingredients:

For the chipotle sauce:
- 1 cup marinara or tomato sauce
- 3/4 cup water
- 1/2 cup chipotle in adobo sauce
- 1 tsp kosher salt

For the omelet:
- 1 tbsp butter
- 1 tbsp jalapeños, diced
- 2 tbsp red onion, diced
- 2 tbsp cilantro, chopped
- 2 tbsp tomatoes, diced
- 1/4 cup fried corn tortillas, cut into strips
- 3 eggs, beaten
- 2 slices cheese
- salt and pepper

For the garnishings:
- 2 oz hot chipotle sauce
- 1/4 cup fried corn tortillas, cut into strips
- 1 tbsp sliced green onions
- 1 tbsp guacamole

Directions:

1. Melt butter in a pan over medium heat, making sure to coat the entire pan.
2. Sauté the jalapeños, cilantro, tomatoes, onions, and tortilla strips for about a minute.
3. Add the eggs, seasoning them with salt and pepper and stirring occasionally.
4. Flip the omelet when it has set. Place the cheese on the top half.
5. When the cheese starts to melt, fold the omelet in half and transfer to a plate.
6. Mix all of the chipotle sauce ingredients together.
7. Garnish the omelet with chipotle sauce, guacamole, green onions, and corn tortillas.

CHAPTER 2: COPYCAT LUNCH RECIPES

CHIPOTLE'S CHICKEN

Preparation Time: 10 min

Marinating Time: 24 hours

Cooking Time: 20 min

Ingredients:

- 2 1/2 lb chicken breasts or thighs, boneless and skinless
- cooking spray

For the marinade:

- 7 oz chipotle peppers in adobo sauce
- 2 tbsp olive oil
- 6 garlic cloves, peeled
- salt and pepper
- 1/2 tsp cumin
- 1/2 tsp dry oregano

Directions:

1. Pour all the marinade ingredients in a food processor and blend until you get a smooth paste.
2. Pound the chicken until it has a thickness between 1/2 to 3/4 inch. Place chicken into an airtight container or plastic bag. Pour the marinade over the chicken and stir until well coated. Place the chicken in the refrigerator and let marinate up to 24 hours.
3. Cook the chicken over medium to high heat in an oiled and preheated grill for 3 to 5 minutes per side. The internal temperature of the chicken should be 165 degrees F before you remove it from the heat.
4. Let rest before serving. If desired, cut into cubes to add to salads.

POPEYE'S FRIED CHICKEN

Preparation Time: 20 minutes

Cooking Time: 45 minutes

Ingredients:

For the breading:
- 3 cups self-rising flour
- 1 cup corn starch
- 3 tbsp salt
- 2 tbsp paprika
- 1 tsp baking soda
- 1 package dry Italian-style salad dressing mix
- 1 package dry onion soup mix
- 1 packet dry spaghetti spices and seasoning sauce mix
- 3 tbsp white sugar

For the batter:
5. 3 cups cornflake cereal, crushed
6. 2 eggs, beaten
7. 1/4 cup cold water

For the chicken:
- 2 cups oil, for frying
- 1 whole chicken, cut into pieces

Directions:

1. Preheat the oven to 350 degrees F.
2. Mix all of the breading ingredients together in a deep bowl.
3. Place the crushed cereal in another bowl.
4. In a 3rd bowl, beat the eggs and cold water together.
5. Heat the oil to 350 degrees F in a large skillet.
6. Dip the chicken into the breading mixture, the egg mixture, the crushed cereal, and then the breading mixture again.
7. Immediately place the breaded chicken into the heated oil and cook on each side for 3 to 4 minutes.
8. Place the chicken in a 9×13 baking pan skin-side up. Cover the baking pan with foil, leaving a small opening.
9. Bake the chicken for 45 minutes.
10. After 45 minutes, remove the foil and continue baking for another 5 minutes.
11. Remove the baking pan from the oven and serve.

MCDONALD'S CHICKEN NUGGETS

Preparation Time: 15 minutes

Cooling Time: 2 hours

Cooking Time: 45 minutes

Ingredients:

For the chicken:
- 1-pound chicken tenderloins, boneless and thawed

For the brine:
- 4 cups water, cold
- 2 tsp salt

For the breading:
- 1/3 + 1/2 cup all-purpose flour, sifted
- 1/2 cup corn starch
- 1 1/2 tbsp salt
- 1 tbsp fine corn flour
- 1 1/2 tsp dry milk powder, non-fat
- 1 tsp granulated sugar
- 1/2 tsp ginger, ground
- 1/4 tsp mustard, ground
- 1/4 tsp black pepper, fine
- 1/4 tsp white pepper, fine
- 1/8 tsp allspice, ground
- 1/8 tsp cloves, ground
- 1/8 tsp paprika, ground
- 1/8 tsp turmeric, ground
- 1 pinch cinnamon, ground
- 1 pinch cayenne pepper

For the batter:
- 2 eggs, beaten
- 1/2 cup water, cold
- 2 tbsp corn starch
- 2 tbsp all-purpose flour
- 1/4 tsp sea salt, fine
- 1/4 tsp sesame oil
- 1/4 tsp soy sauce
- 1/4 tsp granulated sugar

For deep frying:
- vegetable oil, 3 parts
- vegetable shortening, 1 part

Directions:

1. Pound the chicken until it is only 1/2 inch thick.
2. Mix the brine ingredients.
3. Cut the chicken into nugget-sized pieces and place them in the brine. Leave in the refrigerator for 2 hours.
4. When the chicken is almost done soaking, whisk together all the batter ingredients. Also mix together all the breading ingredients.
5. Remove the chicken from the refrigerator and evenly coat each piece with the batter.
6. Evenly coat each battered piece with the breading.
7. Slowly heat the deep-frying ingredients to 350 degrees F.
8. Deep fry each nugget and then transfer to a plate with a paper towel to drain the oil.

CHILI'S BABY BACK RIBS

Preparation Time: 15 minutes

Cooking Time: 3 hours 30 minutes

Ingredients:
- 4 racks baby-back pork ribs

For the sauce:
- 1 1/2 cups water
- 1 cup white vinegar
- 1/2 cup tomato paste
- 1 tbsp yellow mustard
- 2/3 cup dark brown sugar packed
- 1 tsp hickory flavored liquid smoke
- 1 1/2 tsp salt
- 1/2 tsp onion powder
- 1/4 tsp garlic powder
- 1/4 tsp paprika

Directions:
1. Mix together all of the sauce ingredients in a pan on a medium heat and bring to a boil.
2. When the sauce starts to boil, reduce to a simmer. Continue simmering the mixture for 45 to 60 minutes, mixing occasionally. When the sauce is almost done, preheat the oven to 300 degrees F.
3. Choose a flat surface and lay some aluminum foil over it, enough to cover 1 rack of ribs. Place the ribs on top.
4. Remove the sauce from heat and brush over the ribs.
5. When the rack is completely covered, wrap it with the aluminum foil and place it on the baking pan with the opening of the foil facing upwards.

6. Bake the ribs for 2 1/2 hours.
7. When they are almost done baking, preheat your grill to medium heat.
8. Grill both sides of each rack for 4 to 8 minutes. When you are almost done grilling, brush some more sauce over each side and grill for a few more minutes. Make sure that the sauce doesn't burn.
9. Transfer the racks to a large plate and serve with extra sauce.

APPLEBEE'S HONEY BARBECUE SAUCE WITH RIBLETS

Preparation Time: 20 minutes

Cooking Time: 2 - 5 hours

Ingredients:

For the honey barbecue sauce:
- 1 cup ketchup
- 1/2 cup corn syrup
- 1/2 cup honey
- 1/4 cup apple cider vinegar
- 1/4 cup water
- 2 tbsp molasses
- 2 tsp dry mustard
- 2 tsp garlic powder
- 1 tsp chili powder
- 1 tsp onion powder

For the meat:
- 2 1/4 lb pork riblets
- salt and pepper
- garlic
- 1/4 tsp liquid smoke flavoring
- 1 tsp water

Directions:

1. Season the riblets with the salt, garlic, and pepper, sear them on a grill until the meat starts to separate from the bone.
2. Preheat the oven to 275 degrees F.
3. Mix the water and liquid smoke flavoring in a deep pan and place the ribs on an elevated rack inside, making sure that the liquid does not touch the ribs.
4. Cover the pan with two layers of foil and bake for 2 to 5 hours, depending on the strength of your oven. Make sure that the internal temperature of the meat reaches 155 degrees F.
5. While waiting for the riblets to cook, prepare the sauce by mixing all of the sauce ingredients together. Add to a medium heat and simmer for 20 minutes.
6. When the sauce is done cooking, transfer to a bowl and set aside.
7. When the ribs are done cooking, sear them on a grill until the marrow starts sizzling.
8. Place the ribs on a plate and cover generously with the sauce.
9. Serve and enjoy.

CRACKER BARREL'S GREEN BEANS WITH BACON

Preparation Time: 10 minutes

Cooking Time: 45 minutes

Ingredients:
- 1/4 lb sliced bacon, cut into 1 inch pieces
- 3 cans green beans, with liquid
- 1/4 yellow onion, peeled, chopped
- 1 tsp granulated sugar
- salt and pepper

Directions:
1. Half cook the bacon in a saucepan, make sure it does not get crispy.
2. Add the green beans with the liquid to the bacon and season with salt, pepper, and sugar.
3. Top the green beans with the onion and then cover the pan until the mixture boils.
4. Lower the heat and allow the mixture to simmer for another 45 minutes before serving.

CAFÉ RIO'S PORK

Preparation Time: 10 minutes
Cooking Time: 9 hours

Ingredients:

For the marinade:

- 3 lb boneless pork loin
- 12 oz Coca Cola
- 1/4 cup brown sugar

For the seasoning:

- 1 tsp garlic salt
- 1 tsp onion salt
- 1 tsp chili powder
- 1 tsp cumin, ground
- 12 oz Coca Cola

For the sauce:

- 12 oz Coca Cola
- 3/4 cup brown sugar
- 1/2 tsp chili powder
- 1/2 tsp ground cumin
- 1 can green chili, ground
- 1 can red enchilada sauce

Directions:

1. Make the marinade by mixing 12 oz Coca Cola and 1/4 cup sugar in an airtight container or sealable plastic bag.
2. Add the pork and allow to marinate for at least 8 hours.
3. Place the pork into a slow cooker and cover with all of the seasoning ingredients in the order specified. Cook the pork on low for 7 to 9 hours.

4. After cooking, shred the pork and remove the liquid from the slow cooker.
5. Return the shredded pork to the slow cooker.
6. Place all of the sauce ingredients in a food processor. Blend well to create the sauce.
7. Pour the sauce over the pork, and then cook the for another 30 minutes.
8. Transfer to a bowl and serve.

RUBY TUESDAY'S SONORA CHICKEN PASTA

Preparation Time: 25 minutes

Cooking Time: 20 minutes

Ingredients:

For the cheese mixture:
- 1 lb American cheese
- 1/2 cup heavy cream
- 2 tsp olive oil
- 2 tbsp red chili peppers, minced
- 2 tbsp green chili peppers, minced
- 2 tbsp onions, minced
- 1/2 garlic clove, minced
- 2 tbsp water
- 1/4 tsp salt
- 2 tsp sugar
- 1/2 tbsp vinegar
- 1/4 tsp cumin

For the beans:
- 1 can black beans, with water
- 2 tbsp green chili peppers, minced
- 2 tbsp onions, minced
- 1/2 garlic clove, minced
- 1/4 tsp salt
- 1 dash paprika

For the chicken seasoning:
- vegetable oil
- 1/2 tsp salt
- 1 dash dried thyme

- 1 dash dried summer savory
- 4 chicken breast halves, boneless, skinless

For the pasta:
- 1 box penne pasta
- 16 cups water
- 1 tbsp butter

For the garnishings:
- green onion, chopped
- tomatoes, diced

Directions:

1. Preheat grill to 375 degrees F.
2. Start by making the cheese mixture by adding the American cheese and cream to a pan over medium heat and mix until smooth.
3. In another pan, heat the olive oil and sauté the peppers, onions, and garlic clove.
4. After 2 minutes, add the water and bring to a simmer for another 2 minutes.
5. Add the sautéed vegetables to the cheese and continue simmering over low heat. Add in salt, sugar, vinegar, and cumin, and leave the entire mixture over low heat. Continue to stir.
6. Next, make the beans by heating a pan over a medium heat and adding the beans, peppers, onions, garlic, salt, and paprika.
7. When the bean mixture starts boiling, reduce the heat to low and keep it simmering.
8. Mix all the seasoning ingredients and then rub over the chicken.
9. Cook the chicken in oil thoroughly, for 5 minutes on each side, and then slice the chicken pieces into 1/2 inch slices.
10. Boil the pasta in the water. When it is cooked, drain the pasta and mix in the butter while still hot.
11. Assemble the dish by covering the pasta in cheese sauce, placing the bean mixture over it, and then adding the chicken. Garnish the dish by topping with the tomatoes and green onions.

OLIVE GARDEN'S PARMESAN CRUSTED CHICKEN

Preparation Time: 15 minutes
Cooking Time: 40 minutes

Ingredients:

- 1 cup milk
- 2 chicken breasts
- vegetable oil, for frying
- 2 cups cooked linguini pasta
- 2 tbsp butter
- 3 tbsp olive oil
- 2 tsp crushed garlic
- 1/2 cup white wine
- 1/4 cup water
- 2 tbsp flour
- 3/4 cup half-and-half
- 1/4 cup sour cream
- 1/2 tsp salt
- 1 tsp fresh flat leaf parsley, finely chopped
- 3/4 cup mild Asiago cheese, finely grated

For the breading:

- 1 cup plain breadcrumbs
- 2 tbsp flour
- 1/4 cup grated parmesan cheese

For the garnishing:

- 1 Roma tomato, diced
- parmesan cheese, grated

Directions:
1. Pound the chicken until it flattens to 1/2 inch thick.
2. Mix the breading ingredients in a shallow bowl and place the milk in another.
3. Heat vegetable oil over medium to low heat.
4. Dip the chicken in the breading, then the milk, then the breading again. Immediately place into heated oil.
5. Cook the chicken in the oil until golden brown, about 3-4 minutes per side. Remove the chicken and set aside on a plate lined with paper towels.
6. Create a roux by adding flour to heated olive oil and butter over medium heat.
7. When the roux is done, add the garlic, water, and salt to the pan and stir.
8. Add the wine and continue stirring and cooking.
9. Add the half-and-half and sour cream and stir some more.
10. Add the Asiago cheese and let it melt.
11. Finally, add in the parsley and remove from heat. Add pasta and stir to coat.
12. Divide the pasta between serving plates.
13. Top each dish with the chicken, diced tomatoes, and parmesan cheese before serving.

OLIVE GARDEN'S CHICKEN MARSALA

Preparation Time: 10 minutes

Cooking Time: 40 minutes

Ingredients:

- 2 tbsp olive oil
- 2 tbsp butter
- 4 boneless skinless chicken breasts
- 1 1/2 cups sliced mushrooms
- 1 small clove garlic, thinly sliced
- flour, for dredging
- salt and pepper
- 1 1/2 cups chicken stock
- 1 1/2 cups marsala wine
- 1 tbsp lemon juice
- 1 tsp dijon mustard

Directions:

1. Start by pounding the chicken to about 1/2 inch thick
2. In a large skillet, heat 1 tbsp olive oil and 1 tbsp of the butter over medium-high heat.
3. When the oil is hot, dredge the chicken in flour. Season with salt and pepper on both sides.
4. Cook chicken in batches, about 1 to 2 minutes on each side or until cooked through. Remove from skillet, and place on an oven-proof platter. Keep warm, in the oven.
5. In the same skillet, add 1 tbsp of olive oil. On medium-high heat, sauté mushrooms and garlic until softened. Remove from the pan and set aside.

6. Add the chicken stock and loosen any remaining bits in the pan. On high heat, let reduce by half, about 6-8 minutes. Add Marsala wine and lemon juice and allow reduce by half, about 6–8 minutes. Add the mushrooms and garlic back in the saucepan, and stir in the Dijon mustard. Warm for 1 minute on medium-low heat. Remove from heat, stir in the remaining butter to make the sauce silkier.
7. To serve, pour sauce over chicken, and serve immediately.

CRACKER BARREL'S GREEN CHILI JACK CHICKEN

Preparation Time: 5 minutes

Cooking Time: 20 minutes

Ingredients:

- 1 lb chicken strips
- 1 tsp chili powder
- 4 oz green chilies
- 2 cups Monterey Jack cheese, shredded
- 1/4 cup salsa
- olive oil

Directions:

1. Sprinkle the chicken with the chili powder while heating oil over medium heat.
2. Cook the chicken strips until they are half cooked, and then place the green chilies on top of the chicken. Reduce the heat to low.
3. Cook for 1 to 2 minutes before adding the cheese on top. Keep cooking the chicken and cheese until the cheese melts and chicken is cooked through.
4. Serve the chicken with the salsa.

P.F. CHANG'S CRISPY HONEY CHICKEN

Preparation Time: 20 minutes

Marinating Time: 2 hour 20 minutes

Cooking Time: 2 hours

Ingredients:

- 1 lb chicken breast, boneless and skinless, cut into medium sized chunks
- vegetable oil, for frying and deep frying

For the batter:

- 1 cup all-purpose flour
- 1/2 cup cornstarch
- 1 egg
- 3/4 water
- 1/8 tsp baking powder
- 1/8 tsp baking soda

For the chicken seasoning:

- 1 tbsp light soy sauce
- 1/8 tsp white pepper
- 1/4 tsp kosher salt
- 1 tbsp cornstarch

For the sauce:

- 1/2 cup sake or rice wine
- 1/2 cup honey
- 1/3 cup rice vinegar
- 3 tbsp light soy sauce
- 6 tbsp sugar
- 1/4 cup cornstarch
- 1/4 cup water

Directions:

1. Mix all the batter ingredients together and refrigerate for 2 hours.
2. After 1 hour 40 minutes, mix all the seasoning ingredients together and cover the chicken.
3. Place the chicken in the refrigerator to marinate for at least 20 minutes.
4. Mix all the sauce ingredients, except the cornstarch and water, together and set aside.
5. Place a paper towel on a plate in preparation for draining the oil.
6. Heat your oil to 350 degrees F.
7. When your oil is heated, remove the chicken from the refrigerator and pour the batter over.
8. One by one, lower the coated chicken pieces into the heated oil. Keep them suspended until the batter is cooked.
9. When all the chicken is cooked, place it on the plate covered with the paper towel to cool and drain.
10. Place a pan on a medium heat and add the sauce mixture. Bring to a boil. While waiting for it to boil, mix the cornstarch and water in a separate bowl.
11. Slowly pour the cornstarch mixture into the sauce and continue cooking for 2 minutes, until the sauce thickens.
12. When the sauce thickens, remove it from heat.
13. When the chicken is cooked, pour the sauce over, just enough to cover the chicken.
14. Transfer everything to a plate and serve with rice.

BOSTON MARKET'S CHICKEN POT PIE

Preparation Time: 10 minutes

Cooking Time: 40 minutes

Ingredients:
- 1 cup half-and-half
- 1 cup chicken broth
- 3 tbsp all-purpose flour + extra for rolling
- 2 cups shredded chicken breast, roasted and skinless
- 2 cups mixed frozen vegetables, thawed
- 2 tbsp fresh flat-leaf parsley, chopped
- 2 tbsp chives, chopped
- 1 tsp fresh thyme, chopped
- 1 tsp lemon juice
- 1 tsp salt
- 1/2 tsp lemon zest, grated
- 1/2 tsp freshly ground black pepper
- 7 oz ready-to-use refrigerated pastry

Directions:
1. Preheat oven to 425 degrees F and gather 4 ramekins.
2. Bring the half-and-half, broth, and flour to a boil while stirring with a whisk.
3. Reduce the heat and continue to simmer for another 4 minutes while continuing to whisk the mixture.
4. When the mixture thickens, add the remaining ingredients into the mix, except the pie crust.
5. When all the ingredients are cooked, turn off the heat and cover the pan. Set the mixture aside to work on the pie crust.

6. Lightly flour a flat surface. Place the pastry on your floured surface and roll it into a circle with an 11 inch diameter. Cut into quarters.
7. Scoop the warm chicken mixture into each of the ramekins. Cover the tops with the pie crust, letting it drape over the edges. Slice an X into each of the tops to allow the pie to cook through.
8. Bake the pies for 25 minutes and remove from the oven. Let rest for 10 minutes before serving.

CHIPOTLE'S BARBACOA BURRITO WITH CILANTRO RICE

Preparation Time: 20 minutes

Cooking Time: 7 hours

Ingredients:

For the cilantro rice:

- 1 cup jasmine rice
- 1 tbsp cilantro
- 2 cups water
- 2 tbsp lime juice
- 1 tbsp lemon juice
- 1 tsp orange juice
- 1 tbsp canola oil
- 1 bay leaf
- salt

For the barbacoa:

- 4 lb chuck roast, fat trimmed off
- 2 bay leaves
- 2 tsp salt
- 2 tbsp extra virgin olive oil

For the sauce:

- 1/4 cup lime juice
- 1 cup chicken broth
- 1/2 cup apple cider vinegar
- 1 can chipotle peppers in adobo sauce
- 4 tsp ground cumin
- 1/8 tsp ground clove
- 1 tsp black pepper
- 1 tbsp dried oregano garlic cloves

For the burrito:

- 12 large flour tortillas

For the garnishing:

- pico de gallo, optional
- guacamole, optional
- sour cream, optional

Directions:

1. Once you have trimmed any visible fat off the roast, slice into 8 cuts.
2. Coat the cuts with a tsp of salt and set aside.
3. Using the blender, put in all the sauce ingredients and process until smooth. Set aside.
4. Place a thick bottomed pan on the stove and heat over medium-high flame. Once hot, pour in the olive oil.
5. Sear the chunks of beef. Make sure all sides are browned.
6. Transfer the seared chunks to a slow cooker.
7. Pour the prepared sauce on top of the beef and put in the bay leaves.
8. Cover the slow cooker and cook the beef on high for 6 hours.
9. One hour before the appropriate time, shred the beef chucks into strips using two forks. Season the sauce with more salt. Cover and let cook for another hour.
10. Prepare the rice by placing the water in a medium saucepan and bring to a boil. Add the rice and stir in the bay leaf and salt.
11. Once boiling, reduce the flame and let simmer. Cover for about 15 minutes.
12. Remove from flame and leave covered for 5 minutes.
13. Remove bay leaf and fluff rice with a fork.
14. Stir in the citrus juices and canola oil. Add the cilantro on top.
15. Create the burrito by laying the tortilla flat. Place the cilantro rice on and top with the barbacoa. Top with optional extras.
16. Roll the tortilla and serve immediately.

NAKED CHICKEN BURRITO

Preparation Time: 20 minutes
Marinating Time: 5 hours
Cooking Time: 10 minutes

Ingredients:
- 4 chicken thighs, skinless and boneless
- 1/2 red onion, diced
- 1 1/2 cups frozen corn
- 1 tsp ground cumin
- 1/2 tsp dried oregano
- 1 tsp dried onions
- 2 tsp chili powder
- 1 tsp garlic powder
- salt and pepper
- 1 tbsp vegetable oil
- juice of 1 lime
- 1 cup cooked white rice
- guacamole

Directions:
1. Put the chicken thighs in a plastic bag.
2. Pour in the oil, seal the bag, and shake until the chicken is thoroughly coated with oil.
3. Open the bag and add the garlic powder, chili powder, ground cumin, dried onions, dried oregano, salt and black pepper.
4. Seal the bag. Toss bag to allow the spices to coat the chicken.
5. Place in the refrigerator overnight or at least 5 hours.
6. Once the chicken is ready, preheat grill.

7. Grill the chicken for about 5 minutes on each side or until completely cooked through. Set aside and let cool.
8. Prepare the corn salsa by combining the onion and corn in a bowl. Pour in the lime juice. Mix well and season with salt and pepper.
9. Once the chicken is cool, slice it into cubes.
10. Assemble by dividing the cup of rice into four bowls.
11. Top with chicken cubes, corn, salsa, and guacamole.

ITALIAN GARLIC CHICKEN PASTA

Preparation Time: 10 minutes

Cooking Time: 20 minutes

Ingredients:
- 4 chicken breasts, skinless and boneless
- 1 lb fettuccini pasta, cooked
- 1 1/2 cup + 1 tbsp all purpose flour
- 1/2 lb spinach, whole leaf and stemmed
- 1 red bell pepper, julienned
- 1 tbsp garlic, finely chopped
- 1 cup parmesan cheese, grated
- 1/2 cup white wine
- 3 tbsp + 2 tbsp olive oil
- 2 cups heavy cream
- 2 tsp Italian seasoning
- salt and pepper

Directions:
1. Preheat your oven to 350 degrees F.
2. Using a shallow dish, combine the Italian seasoning, pepper, salt, and 1 1/2 cups flour. Stir well.
3. Dredge the chicken breasts in the flour mixture.
4. Heat 3 tbsp of oil in a skillet over medium high flame.
5. Shaking off any excess flour, cook two chicken breasts at a time until golden brown, about 1-2 minutes on each side.
6. Place the cooked chicken on a baking sheet. Cook the remaining breasts.
7. Once all the chicken breasts are cooked, continue baking them in the oven for about 10-15 minutes.

8. Using a saucepan, heat 2 tbsp of oil and sauté the red pepper and garlic over medium-high heat.
9. After a minute, whisk in a tbsp of flour and wine. Once free of lumps, pour in the cream and spinach. Stir and let boil.
10. Once the spinach is wilted, turn off the flame and immediately whisk in the parmesan cheese.
11. Put the pasta in a mixing bowl and pour on the sauce. Toss to coat thoroughly.
12. Divide the pasta onto four plates. Place a breast of chicken on each plate and top with extra parmesan.
13. Serve immediately.

LOBSTER ROLL WITH HOME MADE MAYONNAISE

Preparation Time: 10 minutes

Cooking Time: 7 minutes

Ingredients:

For the mayonnaise:
- 2 egg yolks
- 1 cup vegetable oil
- 1 tbsp dijon mustard
- 4 tbsp lemon juice
- salt and pepper

For the lobster roll:
- 3/4 lb lobster meat, cooked
- 2 hot dog rolls
- 1 scallion, sliced thinly
- 2 tbsp butter, melted
- handful iceberg lettuce, shredded
- lemon juice
- paprika
- salt and pepper

Directions:
1. Prepare the mayonnaise by placing the lemon juice, egg yolks, and mustard in the food processor.
2. Pulse until thoroughly combined.
3. While continuously processing on low, slowly add the vegetable oil until the mixture emulsifies.
4. Season the mayonnaise with salt and pepper.
5. Cut the lobster meat into 1 inch cubes.

6. Put in just enough mayonnaise to bind the lobster cubes together.
7. Preheat your oven or griddle.
8. Brush the insides of each of the rolls with butter. Grill or bake the rolls until golden.
9. Fill the rolls with hefty layers of lettuce and lobster meat. Top with scallions and a dash of paprika.

MONGOLIAN BEEF

Preparation Time: 10 minutes

Cooking Time: 15 minutes

Ingredients:
- 1 lb flank steak
- 1 tbsp garlic, chopped
- 1/2 tsp ginger, minced
- 2 green onions, diagonally sliced
- 3/4 cup brown sugar
- 1/4 cup cornstarch
- 1/2 cup soy sauce
- 1/2 cup + 2 tsp vegetable oil
- 1/2 cup water

Directions:
1. Using a saucepan, heat 2 tbsp of vegetable oil over low to medium flame.
2. Sauté the ginger then garlic. Immediately add the water and soy sauce to prevent the garlic from burning.
3. Turn up the heat to medium and add the brown sugar. Dissolve the sugar and let the sauce boil until thick for about 2 minutes.
4. Turn off the flame and pour the sauce in a bowl. Set aside.
5. Take your flank steak and slice it against the grain to 1/4 inch thick slices.
6. Dip each of the steak slices in the cornstarch. Each slice should have a thin cornstarch coating on both sides.
7. Let the steak slices sit for about 8-10 minutes to allow the cornstarch to stick.

8. Heat 1/2 cup of oil in a wok over medium heat.
9. Sauté the steak slices in the hot oil for about 2-3 minutes. Stir the slices around until the edges slightly darken.
10. Remove the beef slices using a slotted spoon and place on paper towels to drain excess oil.
11. Discard the used oil in the wok and heat over medium flame.
12. Put the meat back in the wok and let simmer for about a minute.
13. Pour in the ginger sugar sauce and stir to coat the meat.
14. Let simmer and put in the green onion slices.
15. Cook for another minute before removing the onions and steak slices with the slotted spoon. Leave the sauce in the wok or pour in a small bowl.
16. Serve immediately with steaming rice.

P.F. CHANG'S BEEF AND BROCCOLI

Preparation Time: 45 minutes

Cooking Time: 15 minutes

Ingredients:
- 3/4 lb beef round steak, cut into 1/8 inch thick strips
- 3 tbsp vegetable oil
- 1 thin slice of fresh ginger root
- 1 clove garlic, peeled and smashed
- 1 lb broccoli, cut into florets

For the marinade:
- 1/3 cup oyster sauce
- 2 tsp toasted sesame oil
- 1/3 cup sherry
- 1 tsp soy sauce
- 1 tsp white sugar
- 1 tsp corn starch

Directions:
1. Mix the marinade ingredients in a bowl until they have dissolved.
2. Marinate the beef in the mixture for 30 minutes.
3. Sauté the ginger and garlic in hot oil for a minute.
4. When the oil is flavored, remove the garlic and ginger and set aside. Add in the broccoli. Continue cooking the broccoli until tender.
5. When the broccoli is cooked, add in with ginger and garlic and set aside. Pour the beef and the marinade into the same pan, heat until beef is cooked.
6. Pour the broccoli, ginger, and garlic back in and keep cooking for another 3 minutes.
7. Transfer to a bowl or plate and serve.

OUTBACK'S SECRET SEASONING MIX FOR STEAKS

Preparation Time: 5 minutes

Ingredients:
- 4–6 tsp salt
- 4 tsp paprika
- 2 tsp ground black pepper
- 1 tsp onion powder
- 1 tsp garlic powder
- 1 tsp cayenne pepper
- 1/2 tsp coriander
- 1/2 tsp turmeric

Directions:
1. Mix all the seasoning ingredients in a small bowl. Rub the spice blend into the meat on all sides and let rest for 15-20 minutes before cooking.

CHAPTER 3:
COPYCAT DINNER RECIPES

CHEESECAKE FACTORY'S PASTA DI VINCI

Preparation Time: 10 minutes

Cooking Time: 50 minutes

Ingredients:

- 1/2 red onion, chopped
- 1 cup mushrooms, quartered
- 2 tsp garlic, chopped
- 1 lb chicken breast, cut into bite-size pieces
- 3 tbsp butter
- 2 tbsp flour
- 2 tsp salt
- 1/4 cup white wine
- 1 cup cream of chicken soup
- basil leaves, for garnishing
- parmesan cheese, for garnishing
- 1 lb penne pasta, cooked and drained

Directions:

1. Sauté the onion, mushrooms and garlic in 1 tbsp of the butter.
2. When they are tender, remove them from the butter and place in a bowl. Cook the chicken in the same pan.
3. When the chicken is done, transfer it to the bowl containing the garlic, onions, and mushrooms and set aside.
4. Using the same pan, make a roux using the flour and remaining butter over low to medium heat.
5. When the roux is ready, mix in the salt, wine, and cream of chicken mixture. Continue stirring the mixture, making sure that it does not burn.

6. When the mixture thickens, allow to simmer for a few more minutes.
7. Mix in the ingredients that you set aside, and transfer the cooked pasta to a bowl or plate.
8. Pour the sauce over the pasta, garnish with parmesan cheese and basil.

LONGHORN STEAKHOUSE'S MAC & CHEESE

Preparation Time: 20 minutes

Cooking Time: 25 minutes

Ingredients:
- 1 lb cavatappi pasta, cooked
- 2 tbsp butter
- 2 tbsp flour
- 2 cups half-and-half
- 2 oz gruyere cheese, shredded
- 8 oz white cheddar, shredded
- 2 tbsp parmesan cheese, shredded
- 4 oz fontina cheese, shredded
- 1 tsp smoked paprika
- 4 pieces bacon, crispy, crumbled
- 1/2 cup panko bread crumbs

Directions:
1. Make a roux by melting the butter and adding flour over medium heat.
2. When the roux is cooked, add in the half-and-half 1/2 cup at a time, adding more as the sauce thickens.
3. Slowly add the cheeses, really allowing each ingredient to incorporate itself into the sauce. Continue stirring the mixture until everything is heated.
4. Place the pasta in a greased 13×9 baking pan. Sprinkle the bacon and panko bread crumbs over the top of the pasta.
5. Bake the pasta in an oven at 350 degrees F for 20-25 minutes, or until breadcrumbs start to become golden brown.

FAZOLI'S BAKED GARLIC CHICKEN SPAGHETTI

Preparation Time: 15 minutes

Cooking Time: 45 minutes

Ingredients:

For the batter:
- 1/2 cup biscuit mix
- 2 tbsp parmesan cheese, grated
- 1 tsp basil
- 1 tsp oregano
- 1/2 tsp garlic powder
- 1/4 tsp pepper

For the chicken:
- 2 tbsp olive oil
- 4 boneless chicken breast halves
- 1 cup mozzarella cheese

For the pasta:
- 4 cups tomato sauce
- 1 can spaghetti sauce
- 3–5 garlic cloves, minced
- 3 cups mozzarella cheese, shredded
- 12 oz linguine, cooked, drained

Directions:

1. Preheat the oven to 350 degrees F and oil a 13×9 baking pan with 1 tbsp of olive oil
2. Preheat a skillet over medium-high heat
3. Mix all of the batter ingredients together thoroughly. Dip the chicken breasts into the batter, covering each completely.
4. Place the remaining olive oil into a pan and brown the chicken on each side.
5. Mix the tomato sauce, spaghetti sauce, and garlic in a separate bowl.
6. Cover the bottom of the baking pan with 1/3 of the pasta. Spread 1/4 of the shredded mozzarella over the pasta as the second layer. Spread 1 cup of the sauce over the second layer.
7. Repeat until all you have left is a little sauce.
8. Place the chicken on top of everything and cover with the remaining sauce.
9. Bake the pasta for 30 minutes, then top with the 1 cup of remaining mozzarella cheese.
10. Bake for another 10 minutes, slice, and serve.

APPLEBEE'S HONEY GRILLED SALMON

Preparation Time: 10 minutes

Cooking Time: 30 minutes

Ingredients:

For the honey pepper sauce:
- 3/4 cup honey
- 1/3 cup soy sauce
- 1/4 cup dark brown sugar, packed
- 1/4 cup pineapple juice
- 2 tbsp fresh lemon juice
- 2 tbsp white distilled vinegar
- 2 tsp olive oil
- 1 tsp black pepper, ground
- 1/2 tsp cayenne pepper
- 1/2 tsp paprika
- 1/4 tsp garlic powder

For the fish:
- 4 8oz salmon fillets, skinned
- vegetable oil
- salt and pepper

Directions:
1. Cook all of the sauce ingredients over medium to low heat until boiling. Once the mixture boils, lower the heat a little and allow it to simmer for another 15 minutes.
2. Rub the salmon with vegetable oil, salt, and pepper, and grill for 4 to 7 minutes on each side.
3. Serve with the honey pepper sauce.

RED LOBSTER'S MAPLE-GLAZED SALMON AND SHRIMP

Preparation Time: 10 minutes

Cooking Time: 20 minutes

Ingredients:

- 2/3 cup maple syrup
- 1/2 cup water
- 2 tbsp dried cherries, minced
- 1 tbsp sugar
- 2 tsp soy sauce
- 1 1/2 tsp lemon juice
- 24 pieces fresh medium shrimp, peeled
- 24 oz salmon fillets
- salt and pepper

Directions:

1. Start by putting 6 shrimp on each skewer and season with salt and pepper.
2. Season the salmon with salt and pepper.
3. Combine the maple syrup, water, cherries, sugar, soy sauce, and lemon juice and bring to a boil over medium heat. Reduce the heat and allow the mixture to simmer for another 8 to 10 minutes.
4. Grill the shrimp over high heat for 1 to 2 minutes per side. When you're done with the shrimp, grill the salmon over high heat for 3 to 4 minutes per side.
5. Arrange the shrimp and salmon on a plate and serve with sauce.

CHILI'S GARLIC AND LIME SHRIMP

Preparation Time: 5 minutes

Cooking Time: 20 minutes

Ingredients:

For the shrimp:

- 2 tbsp butter
- 1 clove garlic, chopped
- 32 pieces fresh medium shrimp, peeled
- juice of 1 lime juice

For the seasoning:

- 3/4 tsp salt
- 1/4 tsp ground black pepper
- 1/4 tsp cayenne pepper
- 1/4 tsp dried parsley flakes
- 1/4 tsp garlic powder
- 1/4 tsp paprika
- 1/8 tsp dried thyme
- 1/8 tsp onion powder

Directions:

1. Stir all the seasoning ingredients together, set aside.
2. Sauté the garlic in the butter over medium heat for a few seconds before adding the shrimp to the pan. Squeeze the lime over the shrimp and continue to sauté.
3. Stir in the seasoning mix, and continue sautéing the mixture for another 5 to 8 minutes.
4. Transfer to a plate and serve with thin lime wedges.

RED LOBSTER'S NANTUCKET BAKED COD

Preparation Time: 10 minutes

Cooking Time: 30 minutes

Ingredients:

For the fish:

- 4 fresh cod fish fillets
- 1 tbsp butter, melted
- 1/2 lemon, juiced
- 2 small tomatoes, sliced
- 2 tbsp grated parmesan cheese

For the spice blend:

- 1/4 tsp salt
- 1/4 tsp paprika
- dash black pepper
- dash cayenne pepper

Directions:

1. Preheat the oven to 450 degrees F and prepare a 9×13 baking pan.
2. Place all the ingredients for the spice blend in a bowl and mix thoroughly.
3. Place the cod filets in the baking pan and brush the tops with butter.
4. Sprinkle the lemon juice and spice blend over the filets.
5. Place 2 to 3 tomato slices on top of the spices for each fish.
6. Cover each slice of tomato with parmesan cheese.
7. Bake the fish for 8 minutes, then broil it on high for another 6 to 8 minutes.
8. Transfer the fish to a serving dish and serve with rice.

CHILI'S CRUNCHY FRIED SHRIMP

Preparation Time: 10 minutes

Cooking Time: 1 hour

Ingredients:
- 2 lb large shrimp, peeled
- vegetable shortening, melted
- corn flake crumbs

For the batter:
- 2/3 cup flour
- 1 1/3 cups cornstarch
- 1/2 tsp salt
- 1/2 tsp baking powder
- 6 egg whites
- 2/3 cup water
- 4 tbsp vegetable oil

Directions:
1. Mix the batter ingredients together and set aside.
2. In a separate container, pour in the cornflake crumbs.
3. Preheat the oil over medium heat.
4. Coat each shrimp with a generous amount of batter and then roll in the crumbs.
5. Deep fry the shrimp until golden brown.
6. Place the shrimp on paper towels to drain oil.

APPLEBEE'S GARLIC AND PEPPERCORN FRIED SHRIMP

Preparation Time: 5 minutes

Cooking Time: 30 minutes

Ingredients:

- 1 lb shrimp, peeled, deveined and tail removed
- vegetable oil, as needed
- 2 eggs, beaten

For the flour mixture:

- 1/2 cup wheat flour
- 1/4 tsp salt
- 1 tsp ground black pepper
- 1 tsp granulated garlic
- 1/2 tsp paprika
- 1 tsp granulated sugar

For the breading:

- 1 cup breadcrumbs
- 1 tsp ground black pepper

Directions:

1. Heat 3 inches of oil to 350 degrees F.
2. Place the ingredients for the flour mixture in a bowl and mix.
3. In a separate bowl, beat the eggs.
4. In a 3rd bowl mix the breading ingredients together.
5. Dip the shrimp in the flour mixture, then the eggs, then the breading.
6. After dipping, place the shrimp directly into the heated oil and cook for 2 to 3 minutes.

BUBBA GUMP SHRIMP COMPANY'S CAJUN SHRIMP

Preparation Time: 5 minutes

Cooking Time: 15 minutes

Ingredients:
- 2 tsp paprika
- 1 tsp dried thyme
- 1/2 tsp salt
- 1/4 tsp nutmeg, ground
- 1/4 tsp garlic powder
- 1/8 tsp cayenne pepper
- 1 tbsp olive oil
- 1 lb medium-sized shrimp, peeled and deveined

Directions:
1. Sauté all the ingredients, except for the shrimp, in oil for 30 seconds.
2. When the ingredients have heated up, add the shrimp and continue sautéing for 2 to 3 minutes.
3. When the shrimp is cooked entirely, transfer to a plate and serve.

RED LOBSTER'S SHRIMP PASTA

Preparation Time: 5 minutes
Cooking Time: 30 minutes

Ingredients:

- 8 oz linguini
- 1/3 cup extra virgin olive oil
- 3 garlic cloves
- 1 lb shrimp, peeled, deveined
- 2/3 cup chicken broth
- 1/3 cup white wine
- 1 cup heavy cream
- 1/2 cup parmesan cheese, freshly grated
- 1/4 tsp dried basil, crushed
- 1/4 tsp dried oregano, crushed
- fresh parsley, for garnishing
- parmesan cheese, for garnishing

Directions:

1. Cook the pasta according to package directions.
2. Simmer the garlic in hot oil over low heat, until tender.
3. Increase the heat to medium and add the shrimp. When cooked, transfer garlic and shrimp to a bowl. Keep the remaining oil in the pan.
4. Pour the chicken broth into the pan and bring to a boil.
5. Add the wine. Keep cooking the mixture for another 3 minutes.
6. While stirring the mixture, reduce the heat to low and add in the cream and 1/2 cup parmesan cheese. Keep stirring.

7. When the mixture thickens, return the shrimp to the pan and add the basil and oregano.
8. Place the pasta in a bowl and pour the sauce over it.
9. Mix everything together and serve. Garnish with parsley and parmesan cheese, if desired

OLIVE GARDEN'S STEAK GORGONZOLA

Preparation Time: 10 minutes

Cooking Time: 1 hour 30 minutes

Ingredients:

- 2 1/2 lb boneless beef top sirloin steaks, cut into 1/2 inch cubes
- 1 lb linguini
- 2 tbsp sun-dried tomatoes, chopped
- 2 tbsp balsamic vinegar glaze
- fresh parsley leaves, chopped

For the marinade:

- 1 1/2 cups Italian dressing
- 1 tbsp fresh rosemary, chopped
- 1 tbsp fresh lemon juice

For the spinach gorgonzola sauce:

- 4 cups baby spinach, trimmed
- 2 cups Alfredo sauce
- 1/2 cup green onion, chopped
- 6 tbsp gorgonzola, crumbled and divided

Directions:

1. Cook the pasta and set aside.
2. Mix together the marinade ingredients in a sealable container.
3. Marinate the beef in the container for an hour.
4. While the beef is marinating, make the spinach gorgonzola sauce. Start by heating the Alfredo sauce in a saucepan over medium heat. Add spinach and green onions. Let simmer until the spinach wilts. Crumble 4 tbsp of the gorgonzola cheese on top of the sauce. Let melt and stir. Set aside remaining 2 tbsp of the cheese for garnish. Set aside and cover with lid to keep warm.

5. When the beef is done marinating, grill each piece depending on your preference.
6. Toss the cooked pasta into the Alfredo sauce, and then transfer to a plate.
7. Top the pasta with the beef, and garnish with balsamic glaze, sun-dried tomatoes, crumbled gorgonzola cheese, and parsley leaves.
8. Serve and enjoy.

NOODLES AND COMPANY'S PAD THAI

Preparation Time: 5 minutes
Cooking Time: 20 minutes

Ingredients:

For the sauce:

- 1/2 cup boiling water
- 1/4 cup brown sugar
- 6 tbsp lime juice
- 1/4 cup rice vinegar
- 1/4 cup Thai fish sauce
- 2 tsp Sriracha

For the pad Thai:

- 12 ounces dried flat rice noodles
- 2 tbsp canola oil, divided
- 1/2 yellow onion, sliced
- 3 cloves fresh garlic, minced
- 3 eggs, lightly beaten
- 1/2 cup cabbage, sliced
- 1/2 cup mushrooms, sliced
- 1 cup carrots, sliced
- 1 cup broccoli, chopped
- cilantro, for garnishing
- sliced green onions, for garnishing
- lime wedges, for garnishing

Directions:

1. Dissolve the brown sugar in the boiling water. When the sugar has completely dissolved, mix in the lime juice, vinegar, fish sauce, and Sriracha.
2. Cook the noodles.
3. Sauté the onion in 1 tbsp of oil over medium to high heat for 1 minute. Add in the garlic and sauté for another 30 seconds. Mix the eggs into the garlic and onion mixture, and continue to cook until the egg is cooked completely.
4. Transfer the egg mixture to a bowl and add the remaining oil to the same pan. Sauté the cabbage, mushrooms, carrots, and broccoli.
5. When the vegetables are crispy, add in half of the sauce and cook for 1 to 3 minutes. When your desired consistency is reached, add in the egg mixture and noodles and transfer to a plate to serve.

SBARRO'S BAKED ZITI

Preparation Time: 5 minutes

Cooking Time: 40 minutes

Ingredients:

- 2 lb ziti pasta
- 1 1/2 lb mozzarella cheese, shredded
- 1 cup roasted garlic-and-onion spaghetti sauce
- cooking spray

For the pasta sauce:

- 2 lb ricotta cheese
- 3 oz Romano cheese, grated
- 3 cups roasted garlic-and-onion spaghetti sauce
- 1/2 tsp black pepper

Directions:

1. Preheat the oven to 350 degrees F and lightly coat a 13×9 baking pan with cooking spray.
2. Cook and drain the pasta according to package instructions.
3. Thoroughly mix together the pasta sauce ingredients.
4. Combine the pasta sauce with the cooked pasta.
5. Spread the 1 cup spaghetti sauce over the bottom of the baking pan.
6. Add the ziti to the sauce and sprinkle everything with the mozzarella cheese.
7. Loosely cover the pasta with aluminum foil and bake for 12 to 15 minutes, or until the cheese is well melted and the edges of the pan are bubbly and golden.
8. Transfer to a plate and serve.

NOODLES AND COMPANY'S INDONESIAN PEANUT SAUTÉ

Preparation Time: 5 minutes

Cooking Time: 30 minutes

Ingredients:
- vegetable oil
- 2 lb chicken, boneless, skinless and cut into thin strips
- 1 package linguine
- 1/2 cup shoestring carrots
- 1/2 cup broccoli florets
- 4-5 green onions, diced finely
- 1 cup bean sprouts
- peanuts, crushed for garnishing
- cilantro, for garnishing
- 2–3 limes, cut into wedges for garnishing
- 2–4 tsp Sriracha

For the marinade:
- 1 tbsp hot sauce
- juice of 1 lime
- 3 cloves garlic, pressed
- 1 tbsp fresh ginger, minced
- 2 tsp soy sauce
- salt and pepper

For the peanut sauce:
- 1 cup chicken broth
- 6 tbsp creamy peanut butter
- 3 tbsp honey
- 6 tbsp soy sauce
- 3 tbsp fresh minced ginger
- 4–5 cloves garlic, pressed or minced

Directions:

1. Mix the marinade ingredients together in a bowl. Add the chicken and let soak 10-15 minutes. Remove chicken.
2. Warm 1-2 tbsp of vegetable oil in a large sauté pan such as a wok. Sauté the chicken in the Sriracha.
3. Cook the pasta al dente according to package directions.
4. Remove the chicken from heat and wrap it in foil to retain its warmth.
5. While waiting for the pasta to cook, make the peanut sauce by mixing all the ingredients in a small saucepan over medium to low heat. Keep cooking and stirring the sauce until it becomes smooth, about 3 minutes.
6. Using the pan you used to cook the chicken, sauté the carrots, broccoli, onions, and beansprouts in oil. Add the beansprouts last so that they do not get overcooked.
7. When the beansprouts are half cooked, add in the chicken and cover. Lower the heat.
8. When the pasta is cooked, drain and transfer them to the pan. Add the peanut sauce and stir to coat.
9. To serve, divide into four bowls. Garnish with cilantro, crushed peanuts, and lime.

OLIVE GARDEN'S STUFFED MUSHROOMS

Preparation Time: 10 minutes

Cooking Time: 45 minutes

Ingredients:

For the stuffed mushrooms:
- 12 fresh mushrooms, de-stemmed, rinsed, and dried
- 1 tsp flat leaf parsley, minced
- 1/4 tsp dry oregano
- 1/4 cup + 1 tbsp butter, melted, cooled
- 1/4 cup mozzarella cheese, finely grated
- fresh parsley, for garnishing

For the stuffing:
- 1 can clams, drained and finely minced, save 1/4 cup of juice
- 1 green onion, finely minced
- 1 egg, beaten
- 1/2 tsp garlic, minced
- 1/8 tsp garlic salt
- 1/2 cup Italian breadcrumbs
- 1 tbsp red bell pepper, finely diced
- 2 tbsp parmesan cheese, finely grated
- 1 tbsp Romano cheese, finely grated
- 2 tbsp mozzarella cheese, finely grated

Directions:

1. Preheat the oven to 350 degrees F and grease a small baking pan.
2. Thoroughly mix all the stuffing ingredients, except clam juice and the cheeses.
3. When everything is blended, add in the clam juice and mix again. Next, add in the cheeses and continue mixing.
4. Stuff each of the mushrooms with about 1 1/2 tsp of the mixture.
5. Pour 1 tbsp of the butter into the baking pan and arrange the mushrooms on the pan. Then mix 1/4 cup of the melted butter with the oregano and the parsley. Pour the butter mixture over the mushrooms.
6. Cover the pan with a lid or foil and bake for 35-40 minutes.
7. Uncover the mushrooms and sprinkle the remaining mozzarella cheese over the top. Bake for another few minutes, until the cheese melts.
8. Transfer to a serving plate. Garnish with parsley.

CRACKER BARREL'S BABY CARROT

Preparation Time: 5 minutes

Cooking Time: 45 minutes

Ingredients:
- 1 tsp bacon grease, melted
- 2 lb fresh baby carrots
- water
- 1 tsp salt
- 1/4 cup brown sugar
- 1/4 cup butter, melted
- 1/4 cup honey

Directions:
1. Heat the bacon grease in a pot. Place the carrots in the grease and sauté for 10 seconds. Cover the carrots with water and add salt.
2. Bring the entire mixture to a boil over medium heat, then reduce the heat to low and allow it to simmer for another 30 to 45 minutes. By this time, the carrots should be half cooked.
3. Remove half the water from the pot and add the rest of the ingredients.
4. Keep cooking until the carrots become tender. Transfer to a bowl and serve.

OLIVE GARDEN'S GNOCCHI WITH SPICY TOMATO AND WINE SAUCE

Preparation Time: 10 minutes

Cooking Time: 40 minutes

Ingredients:

For the sauce:

- 2 tbsp extra virgin olive oil
- 6 fresh garlic cloves
- 1/2 tsp chili flakes
- 1 cup dry white wine
- 1 cup chicken broth
- 2 cans tomatoes
- 1/4 cup fresh basil, chopped
- 1/4 cup butter, cut into 1 inch cubes, chilled
- 1/2 cup parmesan cheese, freshly grated

For the pasta:

- 1 lb gnocchi
- salt and pepper

Directions:

1. Place the olive oil, garlic and chili flakes in a cold pan and cook over medium heat.
2. When the garlic starts turning golden brown, add the wine and broth and bring the mixture to a simmer.
3. After about 10 minutes, the broth should be halved. When that happens, add in the tomatoes and basil and then let the sauce continue simmering for another 30 minutes.

4. Once the sauce has thickened, set it aside to cool for 3 minutes.
5. After 3 minutes, place the sauce in a blender, and add the butter and parmesan. Purée everything together and set aside.
6. Prepare the pasta by boiling the gnocchi in a large pot. When it is cooked, strain the pasta and mix with the sauce. Season with salt and pepper.
7. Transfer everything to a plate and serve.

CHIPOTLE'S SOFRITAS

Preparation Time: 10 minutes
Cooking Time: 25 minutes

Ingredients:

For the Mexican spice mix:

- 1/2 tsp dried oregano leaves
- 2 tsp ancho chili powder
- 1 tsp cumin, ground
- 1/2 tsp coriander, ground
- 1/2 tsp salt

For the sofritas:

- 1 tbsp olive oil
- 1/2 medium onion, diced
- 2 garlic cloves, minced
- 1 tsp chipotle chili in adobo sauce, minced
- 1 tbsp mild hatch chili, diced
- 2 tbsp tomato paste
- 1 package extra firm tofu, drained, dried and crumbled
- 1 cup Mexican beer
- salt and pepper

For the garnishing:

- tortillas
- lime wedges

Directions:
1. Place all the Mexican spice mix ingredients in a container or plastic bag and shake to mix.
2. Sauté the onion and garlic in oil over medium heat for 5 minutes.
3. Mix in both the chilies and the spice mix and sauté for another minute.
4. Pour in the tomato paste and cook for a minute.
5. Add the tofu, beer, salt, and pepper cook for 5 more minutes.
6. Remove the mixture from heat, transfer to a bowl, and serve with tortillas and thin lime wedges.

IN 'N' OUT'S ANIMAL STYLE BURGER

Preparation Time: 15 minutes

Cooking Time: 40 minutes

Ingredients:

For the caramelized onions:

- 2 tbsp vegetable oil
- 2 large onions, finely chopped
- 3/4 tsp salt
- 1/2 cup water

For the special sauce:

- 1/4 cup mayonnaise
- 2 tbsp ketchup
- 1 tbsp sweet pickle relish
- 1/2 tsp white vinegar

For the burger:

- 2 pounds beef chuck, ground
- 4 hamburger buns
- 1/4 cup dill pickles, sliced
- 3/4 cup iceberg lettuce, shredded
- 4 to 8 thin slices tomato
- salt and pepper
- 1/4 cup yellow mustard
- 8 slices American cheese

Directions:

1. Sauté the onions in the oil over medium heat. Season the onions with the salt.
2. Cover, occasionally opening and stirring, until the onions turn golden brown.
3. After 30 minutes, uncover the pan and continue sautéing for another 8 minutes. Make sure that the onions caramelize.
4. Pour the water into the pan, bring the mixture to a simmer, and scrape off the burnt bits from the bottom. Keep cooking the onions until the water evaporates.
5. Transfer the onions to a bowl and set aside.
6. Mix the special sauce ingredients together in a bowl and set aside.
7. Divide the ground beef into 8 equal portions and shape them into patties. Season both sides with salt and pepper.
8. Toast the split-side of the hamburger buns on an oiled griddle.
9. Cook one side of the patties for 3 minutes. After 3 minutes, spread 1 1/2 tsp of mustard on the uncooked side and flip. Place a slice of cheese on the flipped patty and cook for another 2 minutes.
10. Transfer the patties to a plate.
11. Assemble the burgers in the following order, base bun, 1 tbsp special sauce, pickles, lettuce, tomato, 1 tbsp more special sauce, cooked patty with cheese, carmalized onions, cooked patty with cheese, top bun.

CHAPTER 4: COPYCAT DESSERT RECIPES

HOSTESS® SNO BALLS®

Preparation Time: 15 minutes

Cooking Time: 1 hour 10 minutes

Ingredients:

For the cake:
- 3 eggs
- 1 stick butter, unsalted, softened
- 2 tsp baking soda
- 1 tsp of vanilla extract
- 2 cups all-purpose flour
- 1/3 cup cocoa powder
- 2 cups sugar
- 1 1/2 cups milk
- 1/2 tsp salt

For the frosting:
- 1 1/2 cups sugar
- 6 egg whites
- 1 tsp cream of tarter
- 2 cups coconut, shredded
- 1 tsp coconut extract
- 2 tsp vanilla extract
- 1/3 cup water

Directions:

1. Make the cake by creaming butter with the sugar and then gradually add in vanilla and eggs.
2. Whisk flour with the cocoa, baking soda, and salt in a separate large sized bowl.

3. Add half of the dry mixture to the sugar and butter mixture and then add in the milk and the remaining dry mixture.
4. Scoop into a lightly greased muffin tin and bake for 15 minutes at 350 degrees F. Allow to cool at room temperature.
5. Cut a cone from the bottom of every cake and trim the tip off.
6. Make the frosting by beating the egg whites well until soft peaks form.
7. Combine sugar together with cream of tartar and water in a small sized saucepan, bring everything to a boil, over medium heat.
8. Remove the pan from heat and allow to cool at room temperature.
9. Gradually pour the syrup into the egg whites and then add in vanilla and coconut extract.
10. Whip until the mixture is thickened, for 10 more minutes.
11. Process the coconut in a food processor.
12. Replace the cap of the cake, leaving it upside down for the frosting.
13. Generously coat the bottom and sides with a layer of frosting and then add in the coconut sprinkles.

NEW YORK'S SERENDIPITY® FROZEN HOT CHOCOLATE

Preparation Time: 10 minutes

Cooking Time: 30 minutes

Ingredients:
- 1/3 cup milk powder, dry, nonfat
- 3 tbsp Hershey's cocoa powder
- 1/3 cup granulated sugar
- 1 cup milk
- 3 cups ice
- salt

For the toppings:
- semisweet chocolate bar, shaved using a vegetable peeler
- whipped cream

Directions:
1. Combine milk powder together with cocoa, salt, and sugar in a medium sized bowl. Add to a blender with milk and ice. Blend on high settings until the drink is smooth and the ice is entirely crushed.
2. Pour everything into large glasses and top with whipped cream and semisweet chocolate shavings.

AUNT ANNIE'S PRETZELS

Preparation Time: 15 minutes

Rising Time: 30 minutes

Cooking Time: 25 minutes

Ingredients:
- 2-4 tbsp melted butter
- 3 cups all-purpose flour
- 1 cup bread flour
- 2 tbsp baking soda
- 1 1/4 tsp salt
- 2 tbsp brown sugar
- 1 1/4 tsp active dry yeast
- 3 1/2 cups water
- coarse salt

Directions:
1. Pour 1 1/2 cups lukewarm water in a large sized mixing bowl and then sprinkle the yeast on top of it. Stir several times until completely dissolved.
2. Add sugar and salt and stir several times until dissolved.
3. Add in the flours and knead dough for couple of minutes, until smooth and elastic.
4. Allow to rise for 30 minutes.
5. While the dough is rising, mix baking soda with 2 cups of warm water and stir.
6. Once the dough is risen, take a section of the dough and roll into a 1/2 inch thick long rope and shape into a pretzel.
7. Dip the pretzel into the soda solution. Grease a baking sheet and place on pretzels. Bake in a 450 degrees F oven until golden, approx 10 minutes.
8. Brush the baked pretzel with the melted butter. After brushing sprinkle with the coarse salt.

Alternatively for Auntie Anne's Famous Cinnamon Sugar:

1. Make a mixture of cinnamon and sugar in a large sized shallow bowl and melt a butter stick in a separate shallow bowl.

2. First dip the pretzel in butter, make sure both sides of the pretzel are generously coated with the melted butter and then dip into the cinnamon mixture.

PANERA BREAD® PUDDING WITH APPLES, PECANS, AND RAISINS

Preparation Time: 20 minutes

Cooking Time: 30 hour

Ingredients:

- 1/2 cup pecan halves
- 8 baking apples, small, peeled, cored, and sliced thinly
- 1/2 loaf raisin and cinnamon white bread, torn into bite-sized pieces
- 1 tbsp vanilla extract
- 1 large orange, zest and juice
- 1/2 cup brown sugar, packed
- 4 tbsp butter, unsalted
- 1/2 cup blackberry jam

Directions:

1. Preheat your oven to 400 degrees F.
2. Over medium heat in a medium sized saucepan heat the butter until completely melted. Once melted, cook the bread until coated well, for 2 to 3 minutes.
3. Add sugar, orange juice and zest, pecans, and vanilla extract to the bread. Cook until a sauce begins to form, for 2 to 3 more minutes.
4. Layer the bread mixture in a 9x13 inch baking dish, top with the apples and jam. Bake until bubbly, for around half an hour.

TGI FRIDAYS® MUD PIE

Preparation Time: 10 minutes

Freezing Time: 3 hours

Ingredients:
- 2 pints coffee ice cream, slightly softened, divided
- 1 cup chocolate morsels, semisweet
- 1/4 cup heavy whipping cream
- 1 tsp vanilla extract
- 1/4 cup butter
- 1 prepared 6-ounce chocolate crumb crust
- 2 tbsp light corn syrup
- 3/4 cup nuts, chopped
- 1 cup powdered sugar
- whipped cream

Directions:
1. Over low heat settings in a small saucepan heat butter, sugar, morsels, corn syrup, and cream.
2. Continue stirring until the mixture is completely smooth and butter is completely melted.
3. Remove the pan from heat and add in vanilla extract, stir well.
4. Let cool at room temperature.
5. Once cool drizzle 1/3 cup of the chocolate mixture into the bottom of the crust, then sprinkle 1/4 cup of the nuts.
6. Layer on 1 pint of ice cream, using a large spoon.
7. Freeze for a minimum of an hour.
8. Repeat the process with 1/3 cup of the chocolate mixture, ice cream, and 1/4 cup nuts.
9. Drizzle the leftover chocolate mixture and top with leftover nuts.
10. Freeze for 2 hours.
11. Before serving, top with the whipped cream.

TGI FRIDAYS® TENNESSEE WHISKEY CAKE

Preparation Time: 30 minutes

Cooking Time: 35 minutes

Ingredients:
- 1/4 cup milk
- 1/2 cup granulated sugar
- 1/2 cup molasses
- 3 eggs, large
- 1/2 tsp ground cinnamon
- 1 butter stick, unsalted, softened
- 1/4 tsp baking soda
- 1/2 cup brown sugar
- 1/4 cup Jack Daniel's whiskey
- 1 cup flour
- 1/2 tsp baking powder
- 1/4 tsp salt

For garnising:
- candied pecans
- chocolate sauce
- vanilla ice cream

Directions:
1. Preheat your oven to 350 degrees F.
2. Whisk the flour together with cinnamon, baking powder, baking soda, and salt in a large sized bowl.
3. Beat butter using a mixer at medium-high speed until creamy. Slowly add in the sugars, mix well.
4. Add eggs one at a time. Beat well scraping down the sides after every addition. Add in the flour mixture and milk slowly whilst mixing on a low speed.

5. Add in the molasses and mix well on medium-low speed. Add in the whiskey and mix until smooth.
6. Transfer batter onto a lightly greased 10 inch cake pan lined with the parchment paper. Bake for half an hour. Let cool at room temperature.
7. Serve with chocolate sauce, vanilla ice cream, and candied pecans on top.

KRISPY KREME® DOUGHNUTS

Preparation Time: 15 minutes

Rising Time: 1 hour 30 minutes

Cooking Time: 5 minutes

Ingredients:

For the doughnuts:
- 1/2 cup shortening
- 2 eggs, large
- 1 1/2 cups lukewarm milk, overcooked, then cooled
- 1/4 oz packages yeast
- 1/2 cup sugar
- 5 cups all-purpose flour
- vegetable oil
- 1/4 cup water
- 1 tsp salt

For the chocolate frosting:
- 2 cups powdered sugar
- 1/3 cup butter
- 4 oz semisweet chocolate chips
- 1 1/2 tsp vanilla

For the glaze:
- 1 1/2 tsp vanilla
- 2 cups powdered sugar
- 1/3 cup butter
- 4-6 tbsp hot water

Directions:

1. To a large bowl add water and dissolve the yeast in it.
2. Add eggs, 2 cups flour, milk, sugar, salt, and shortening. Beat on low speed for half a minute using a hand mixer, scraping the sides of the bowl regularly.
3. Now, increase the speed to medium, and beat for couple of minutes, scraping the sides of the bowl from time to time. Add in the leftover flour and stir until smooth. Cover and let rise for an hour, until dough has almost doubled in size.
4. Turn the dough onto lightly floured surface; lightly roll around to coat the dough with flour. Roll the dough gently with floured rolling pin to 1/2 inch thick.
5. Using a floured doughnut cutter, cut the dough. Cover and let rise for half an hour, until almost double in size.
6. Once risen heat the vegetable oil to 350 degrees F in a deep fryer. Using a large spatula slide the doughnuts into hot oil.
7. As the doughnuts rise turn them to the surface and fry for a minute on each side until golden brown. Carefully remove from oil and drain.
8. To make the glaze melt the butter over moderate heat settings. Remove from heat and add in vanilla, and powdered sugar. Stir until smooth. Stir in 1 tbsp of water at a time until you get desired consistency.
9. To make the chocolate frosting heat chocolate, and butter over low heat settings for couple of minutes, until chocolate is completely melted. Remove from heat and add in vanilla and powdered sugar. Stir until smooth.
10. Once cool dip them into the glaze and then spread chocolate frosting over the top.

RED LOBSTER® LAVA CAKE

Preparation Time: 15 minutes

Setting Time: 12 hours

Cooking Time: 18 minutes

Ingredients:
- 3 eggs
- 1/2 cup sugar
- 6 oz chocolate chips
- 1/2 cup all-purpose flour
- 3 tbsp cocoa powder
- 3/4 tsp baking powder
- 10 tbsp butter

Directions:
1. Lightly coat six cups with the cooking spray and set them aside. Over medium-low heat settings in a small sized saucepan, heat the chocolate chips until completely melted and smooth.
2. Add butter in small quantities and stir until well incorporated. Add in the sugar and stir well until completely melted and smooth.
3. Transfer the chocolate mixture to a large sized bowl and set aside.
4. Combine flour with baking powder, and cocoa powder in a small sized bowl.
5. Mix the wet and dry mixtures with a hand mixer. Add one egg at a time and mix well for 5 to 6 minutes on medium setting.
6. Transfer the cake batter evenly into already prepared cups.
7. Using plastic wrap cover and freeze overnight.
8. Heat your oven to 375 degrees F.
9. Remove the wrap and bake until the center of the cake is moist and the edges are firm, for 15 to 18 minutes.
10. Remove from oven and allow to cool for 3 to 5 minutes.
11. Serve warm and enjoy.

FAMOUS AMOS® CHOCOLATE CHIP COOKIES

Preparation Time: 10 minutes

Cooking Time: 12 minutes

Ingredients:
- 4 cups all-purpose flour
- 1 egg
- 1 cup packed light brown sugar
- 1 cup vegetable oil
- 2 cups chocolate chips, semisweet
- 1 cup white sugar
- 1 tsp cream of tartar
- 1 tbsp milk
- 1/2 cup walnuts, chopped
- 1 tsp baking soda
- 1 tsp vanilla extract
- 1 cup butter
- 1 tsp salt

Directions:
1. Thoroughly cream egg together with butter, sugars, oil, vanilla, and milk.
2. Add in the remaining ingredients and mix well.
3. Using a spoon drop the batter onto cookie sheets and bake until light in color, for 10 to 12 minutes at 350 degrees F.

MRS. FIELDS® CHOCOLATE CHIP COOKIES

Preparation Time: 10 minutes

Cooking Time: 22 minutes

Ingredients:

- 2 cups chocolate chips, semisweet
- 1/2 tsp baking soda
- 2 eggs, large
- 1 cup firmly packed dark brown sugar
- 2 1/2 cups all-purpose flour
- 1/2 cup white sugar
- 2 tsp pure vanilla extract
- 1 cup cold salted butter, cut into cubes
- 1/4 tsp salt

Directions:

1. Preheat your oven to 300 degrees F.
2. Combine flour together with baking soda, and salt in a medium sized bowl and mix.
3. Blend sugars in a large sized bowl.
4. Add the cold butter to the sugars and mix well to make a grainy paste. Add vanilla extract and eggs and mix with an electric wisk until just blended.
5. Add chocolate chips and flour mix. Blend until just mixed at a low speed. Don't over mix.
6. Drop the batter onto an ungreased cookie sheet using rounded tbsp, 2 inch apart.
7. Bake until golden, for 20 to 22 minutes.
8. Using a large sized spatula, immediately transfer the cookies to a cool surface.

DAVID'S CHOCOLATE CHIP COOKIES

Preparation Time: 10 minutes

Cooking Time: 10 minutes

Ingredients:
- 1 tsp vanilla extract
- 2 eggs, large
- 1 3/4 cups all-purpose flour
- 4 1/2 cups rice cereal, crispy
- 1 cup butter, softened
- 3/4 cup light brown sugar
- 1 tsp baking soda
- 3/4 cup white sugar
- 2 cups chocolate chips, semisweet
- 1/2 tsp salt

Directions:
1. Preheat your oven to 350 degrees F.
2. Add cereal in a blender or food processor and process on high settings until it reaches a fine powder. Measure out a cup of powder and mix it with baking soda, flour, and salt. Set aside.
3. Cream the butter together with brown, and white sugar in a large sized bowl.
4. Beat in the eggs, one at a time, and then add in vanilla, stir well.
5. Slowly blend in the dry ingredients and then add in the chocolate chips, stir well.
6. Using rounded spoonfuls drop the batter onto cookie sheet.
7. Bake in the preheated oven for 8 to 10 minutes.
8. Let the cookies cool for 5 minutes, then remove to a wire rack to completely cool.

THIN MINTS GIRL SCOUT COOKIES

Preparation Time: 20 minutes

Setting Time: 15 minutes

Cooking Time: 10 minutes

Ingredients:

For the chocolate wafers:

- 1 cup cocoa powder, unsweetened
- 1 tsp vanilla extract
- 1 1/2 cups all-purpose flour
- 1 cup powdered sugar
- 1 cup butter
- 3/4 tsp salt

For the chocolate peppermint coating:

- 1 lb semisweet chocolate, chopped
- 1 tsp peppermint extract

Directions:

1. Make the cookie dough by creaming the butter until light and fluffy in a mixer.
2. Add powdered sugar and continue creaming.
3. Stir in the cocoa powder, vanilla extract, and salt. Mix until the batter resembles a thick frosting.
4. Add in the flour and mix until the batter is crumbly.
5. Place the dough onto a clean surface, shape it into a ball, kneading it together.
6. Evenly divide the dough into 2 flattened disks and wrap in plastic wrap.
7. Let chill in a refrigerator for 12 to 15 minutes.
8. Preheat your oven to 350 degrees F.

9. Rollout the dough between two plastic sheets approximately 1/8 inch thin.
10. Cut out the cookies and bake in the preheated oven for 10 minutes.
11. Remove from oven and let the cookies cool completely on wire racks.
12. Make the chocolate peppermint coating by gradually melting the chocolate using a double boiler until glossy and smooth, stirring occasionally. Once melted stir in the peppermint extract.
13. Gently drop the cookies one at a time into the chocolate coating using a fork. Flip several times until all sides of the cookies are coated with the chocolate.
14. Using a fork, lift out the cookie from the chocolate and drain any extra chocolate off the cookie by banging the fork on the side of the pan.
15. Line a large baking sheet with the parchment pepper and place the cookies on them, repeat the process for the remaining cookies. Place them in a refrigerator until set.

PANERA BREAD'S CHOCOLATE CHIP COOKIES

Preparation Time: 15 minutes

Setting Time: 15 minutes

Cooking Time: 15 minutes

Ingredients:

- 2 1/2 sticks unsalted butter
- 1 1/4 cup dark brown sugar
- 1/4 cup granulated sugar
- 2 tsp vanilla extract
- 2 eggs
- 3 1/2 cups all-purpose flour
- 1 tbsp cornstarch
- 1 tsp baking soda
- 1 tsp salt
- 1 bag mini semisweet chocolate chips

Directions:

1. Cream the butter and sugars using a whisk or a hand mixer.
2. Whip in the vanilla extract and eggs and set aside.
3. In a different bowl, mix together the flour, cornstarch, baking soda, and salt.
4. Pour the dry mixture into the wet mixture a little at a time, folding with a spatula. Add in the chocolate chips and continue folding.
5. Roll the cookie dough into balls and place on a baking sheet. Place the baking sheet in the freezer for 15 minutes.
6. Preheat the oven to 350 degrees F while waiting for the cookies to harden.
7. Transfer the cookies from the freezer to the oven immediately and bake for 15 minutes.

APPLEBEE'S MAPLE BUTTER BLONDIE

Preparation Time: 10 minutes

Cooking Time: 25 minutes

Ingredients:
- 1/3 cup butter, melted
- 1 cup brown sugar, packed
- 1 egg, beaten
- 1 tbsp vanilla extract
- 1 cup all-purpose flour
- 1/2 tsp baking powder
- 1/8 tsp baking soda
- 1/8 tsp salt
- 1/2 cup white chocolate chips
- 1/2 cup walnuts or pecans, chopped

For the maple cream sauce:
- 1/2 cup maple syrup
- 1/4 cup butter
- 1/2 cup brown sugar
- 8 oz cream cheese, softened

Directions:
1. Preheat the oven to 350 degrees F and grease an 8×8 baking pan.
2. Dissolve the sugar in the melted butter. Whip in the egg and the vanilla and set the mixture aside.
3. In another bowl, mix together the flour, baking powder and soda, and salt.
4. Slowly pour the dry mixture into the butter mixture and mix thoroughly.
5. Once the mixture is at room temperature, fold in the nuts and chocolate chips.

6. Transfer the mixture into the baking pan and bake for 20 to 25 minutes.
7. While waiting for the blondies to bake, make the maple cream sauce by combining the syrup and butter over low heat. When the butter has melted, mix in the sugar and cream cheese. Take the mixture off the heat when the cream cheese has melted, and set aside.
8. Let the blondies cool a little and then cut into rectangles. Serve with the maple cream sauce.

TOMMY BAHAMA'S KEY LIME PIE

Preparation Time: 20 minutes

Setting Time: 2 hours

Cooking Time: 30 minutes

Ingredients:

For the pie:
- 10 inch graham cracker crust
- 1 egg white
- 2 1/2 cups sweetened condensed milk
- 3/4 cup egg yolk
- 1 cup lime juice
- 1 lime, zest
- 1 lime, sliced into 8

For the white chocolate mousse:
- 8 floz heavy cream
- 3 tbsp powdered sugar
- 1/4 tsp vanilla extract
- 1/2 tbsp white chocolate mousse instant mix

Directions:

1. Preheat the oven to 350 degrees F.
2. Brush the graham cracker crust with the egg white. Cover the crust completely before placing it in the oven to bake for 5 minutes.
3. Whip the egg yolk and condensed milk together until they are blended completely. Add the lime juice and zest to the mixture and continue whipping until the mixture is smooth.
4. When the crust has cooled, add in the mixture and bake at 250 degrees F for 25 to 30 minutes.
5. When the pie is cooked, place it on a cooling rack to cool. Then place it in the refrigerator for at least 2 hours.

6. While waiting for the pie to cool, beat the heavy cream, powdered sugar and vanilla extract for 2 minutes with a hand mixer. When the mixture is smooth, add in the chocolate mousse and beat to stiff peaks.
7. Remove the pie from the refrigerator, slice it into eight pieces, and garnish each with the white chocolate mousse whipped cream and slices of lime.

DAIRY QUEEN'S BLIZZARD

Preparation Time: 5 minutes

Ingredients:
- 1 candy bar of your choice
- 1/4 to 1/2 cup milk
- 2 1/2 cups vanilla ice cream
- 1 tsp fudge sauce

Directions:
1. Place the candy bar of your choice into the freezer to harden it.
2. Once hard break the candy bar into multiple tiny chunks and place all the ingredients into a blender.
3. Keep blending until the ice cream becomes thicker and everything is mixed completely.
4. Pour into a cup and consume.

OLIVE GARDEN'S TIRAMISU

Preparation Time: 10 minutes

Cooking Time: 2 hours 40 minutes

Ingredients:
- 4 egg yolks
- 2 tbsp milk
- 2/3 cup granulated sugar
- 2 cups mascarpone cheese
- 1/4 tsp vanilla extract
- 1 cup heavy cream
- 1/2 cup cold espresso
- 1/4 cup Kahlua
- 20–24 ladyfingers
- 2 tsp cocoa powder

Directions:
1. Bring water to a boil, then reduce the heat to maintain a simmer. Place a heatproof bowl over the water, making sure that the bowl does not touch the water.
2. In the heatproof bowl, whisk together the egg yolks, milk and sugar for about 8 to 10 minutes.
3. When the mixture has thickened, remove the bowl from heat and then whisk in the vanilla and mascarpone cheese until the mixture becomes smooth.
4. In another bowl, whisk the cream until soft peaks are formed.
5. Using a spatula, fold the whipped cream into the mascarpone mixture, making sure to retain the fluffiness of the whipped cream.
6. In another bowl, mix the espresso and Kahlua.
7. Dip the ladyfingers into the espresso mixture one by one. Dip only the bottom, and dip them quickly so as not to make them soggy.

8. Cover the bottom of an 8×8 pan with half of the dipped ladyfingers, cracking them if necessary.
9. Pour half of the mascarpone mixture over the ladyfingers.
10. Place another layer of ladyfingers over the mixture.
11. Pour the rest of the mixture over the second layer of ladyfingers and smooth out the top.
12. Dust some cocoa powder over the top and then place in the refrigerator to set.

CHEESECAKE FACTORY'S OREO CHEESECAKE

Preparation Time: 25 minutes

Cooking Time: 2 hours 15 minutes

Ingredients:

For the crust:

- 1 1/2 cups Oreo cookies, crushed
- 2 tbsp butter, melted

For the filling:

- 3 packs cream cheese, room temperature
- 1 cup sugar
- 5 large eggs, room temperature
- 2 tsp vanilla extract
- 1/4 tsp salt
- 1/4 cup all-purpose flour
- 1 8oz container sour cream, room temperature
- 14 Oreo cookies, divided

Directions:

1. To make the crust, crush Oreos in a blender or smash them with a rolling pin and mix them with the melted butter. Press the Oreo mixture to the bottom and sides of a 9 inch spring form pan.
2. Leave the crust to rest.
3. Preheat the oven to 325 degrees F.
4. Place the cream cheese in a medium-sized bowl and beat it with a hand mixer until it is light and fluffy.
5. Beat in the sugar, mixing continuously so that the sugar is evenly distributed throughout the mixture.

6. Beat in the eggs, one at a time, and then add in the vanilla, salt, and flour. When the ingredients are all mixed together, add in the sour cream and 6 chopped Oreos.
7. Pour the filling onto the crust and then top with 8 whole Oreos.
8. Bake in the oven for 1 hour 15 minutes. When the cake is done baking, leave it in the oven with the door open for an hour.
9. Serve.

TCBY'S CHOCOLATE YOGURT PIE

Preparation Time: 10 minutes

Freezing Time: 8 hours 10 minutes

Cooking Time: 25 minutes

Ingredients:
- 2/3 cup butter
- 1 1/4 cups sugar
- 1 cup unsweetened cocoa powder
- 1/4 tsp salt
- 1/2 tsp vanilla extract
- 2 large eggs
- 1/2 cup all-purpose flour
- 1 pint TCBY chocolate yogurt
- whipped cream
- caramel syrup

Directions:
1. Before you begin, preheat the oven to 325 degrees F.
2. Place a heatproof bowl in simmering water and mix the butter, sugar, cocoa powder, and salt over the heat.
3. Continue stirring and heating the mixture until it becomes smooth. Remove the bowl from the heat and set aside.
4. When the mixture becomes a little cooler, mix in the vanilla extract and the eggs, one at a time.
5. Beat the flour into the mixture with a wooden spoon until the entire mixture is thoroughly blended.
6. Transfer the mixture to a greased baking pan and then bake for 20 to 25 minutes.

7. Remove from the oven and transfer to a cooling rack.
8. When the pie has cooled down, spread frozen yogurt over the surface and freeze for 10 to 15 minutes.
9. Garnish with whipped cream and caramel syrup, and then return to the freezer for at least 8 hours.
10. Cut the pie into equal portions and serve.

CHILI'S CHOCOLATE BROWNIE SUNDAE

Preparation Time: 20 minutes

Cooking Time: 30 minutes

Ingredients:

- 1/2 cup flour
- 1/3 cup cocoa
- 1/4 tsp salt
- 1/4 tsp baking powder
- 1/2 cup margarine, melted
- 1 cup white sugar
- 2 eggs
- 1 tsp vanilla
- 1/2 cup chocolate chips
- 1/2 gallon vanilla ice cream, slightly softened
- 1 jar fudge, for topping
- whipped cream, for topping
- 1/2 cup walnuts, coarsely chopped
- 8 maraschino cherries, for garnishing

Directions:

1. Preheat oven to 350 degrees F. Grease a 9×9 baking pan.
2. Sift together flour, cocoa, baking powder, and salt in a bowl. Set aside.
3. Combine melted margarine, sugar, eggs, and vanilla, blend well.
4. Add flour mixture, stirring briefly to moisten.
5. Stir in chocolate chips.
6. Pour into prepared pan.

7. Bake for around 30 minutes until fragrant and corners begin to separate from pan.
8. Cool slightly before cutting into 8 bars.
9. Place a scoop of ice cream on top of each brownie and drizzle with fudge sauce.
10. Top with whipped cream, and sprinkle with chopped walnuts.
11. Garnish with cherries.

BEN & JERRY'S CHERRY GARCIA ICE CREAM

Preparation Time: 5 minutes

Chilling Time: 2 hours

Churning Time: 20 minutes

Freezing Time: 4 hours

Ingredients:

- 1/4 cup cherries, fresh or frozen, drained well and rough chopped
- 2 cups thick cream
- 1 cup milk
- 3/4 cup sugar
- 2 large eggs
- 1/4 cup semisweet chocolate, broken into bits

Directions:

The steps in making ice cream vary depending on the type of ice cream maker used. Below are the basic steps, but it's best to follow the manufacturer's instructions.

1. In a saucepan, whisk together cream, milk, sugar, and eggs.
2. Whisk while heating gently to 165 degrees F. Remove from heat.
3. Strain into a bowl.
4. Cover and let chill for 2 hours.
5. Place in ice cream maker and let churn. It should be ready in about 20 minutes.
6. Add cherries and chocolate just before ice cream is done.
7. Transfer to containers, cover, and freeze for around 4 hours.
8. Serve and enjoy.

TGI FRIDAY'S OREO MADNESS

Preparation Time: 10 minutes

Freezing Time: 2 hours

Ingredients:
- 1 pack Oreo cookies
- 1/2 cup butter, melted
- 5 cups vanilla ice cream
- hot fudge, for drizzling
- caramel toppings, for drizzling

Directions:
1. Line muffin tin with cupcake liners.
2. Place Oreos in a food processor and pulse to break into crumbs.
3. Transfer to a bowl and stir in melted butter. Mix well.
4. Press about 2 tbsp each of crumb mixture into muffin tins.
5. Top each with about 1/4 cup ice cream, smoothening down with a spatula.
6. Cover with another 2 tbsp of crumbs.
7. Cover and freeze for about 2 hours.
8. Remove from muffin tins.
9. Drizzle with hot fudge and caramel and serve.

MAGNOLIA BAKERY'S VANILLA CUPCAKES

Preparation Time: 20 minutes

Cooking Time: 25 minutes

Ingredients:

- 1 1/2 cups self-rising flour
- 1 1/4 cups cake flour
- 2 cups granulated sugar
- 1 cup unsalted butter, cubed
- 1 cup whole milk
- 1 tsp pure vanilla extract
- 4 large eggs, lightly beaten

For the frosting:

- 1 cup unsalted butter
- 1 tsp vanilla extract
- 4 cups powdered sugar
- 2 tbsp whole milk + 1 tbsp more if needed

Directions:

1. Preheat oven to 350 degrees F. Line cupcake pan with paper liners.
2. In a large bowl, combine the self-rising flour, cake flour, and sugar. Use an electric mixer and mix at low speed to blend.
3. Add butter, one cube at a time, until batter looks coarse.
4. Stir vanilla into milk and add to batter alternately with eggs, still at slow speed.
5. Fill the cupcake pans about 3/4 full.
6. Bake for 20-25 minutes until a toothpick comes out clean.
7. Place on wire rack and allow to cool completely.
8. Prepare frosting. Cream the butter and add vanilla. Keep mixing while adding sugar a cup at a time. Add milk and mix until creamy. If too thick, add more milk, a drop at a time. Use a spatula or piping bag to frost the cupcakes.

CONCLUSION

Thank you for making it to the end of this copycat cookbook. These recipes are the perfect additions to your daily meals. If you want affordable restaurant-style food, then here is the answer.

We've got recipes from all your favorite restaurants. If you just love having restaurant food at home, then try making some yourself—you never know, you might even be a better cook!

Most of all, the recipes here are meant for you to experience the fulfillment of seeing the smiles on the people with whom you share your creations. Keep trying and having fun with the recipes!

Made in the USA
San Bernardino, CA
08 July 2019